DIPTERA • DANIEL WILLIAM COQUILLET

PROCEEDINGS OF THE WASHINGTON ACADEMY OF SCIENCES. Vol. II, Pp. 389-464. December 7, 1900. PAPERS FROM THE HARRIMAN ALASKA EXPEDITION. IX. ENTOMOLOGICAL RESULTS (8): DIPTERA.

By D. W. Coojjillett. The series of Dipterous insects collect-ed by Professor Trevor Kincaid while a member of the Harriman Expedition to Alaska during the summer of 1899 is one of the most interesting and valuable collections of insects of that order that the U. S. National Museum has acquired for many years. The specimens them-selves, almost without exception, are in first-class condition, and each is accom-panied by a label giving the exact local-ity and date of capture.

The collection contains 2,423 speci-mens, representing 276 species, distrib-uted in 138 genera and 36 families. One genus and 63 of the species are believed to be new to science, and are described in this paper. In addition to the speci-mens referred to above, there are a num-ber of others which it is quite impossi-ble to correctly classify in the present condition of the science; these are chiefly female specimens belonging to groups in which the sexes are very dis-similar in appearance, and the principal classificatory characters are present in the male sex alone, obscure groups which have not as yet been thoroughly studied in this country, and for the prop-er elucidation of which several years of careful study will be required.

Proc. Wash. Acad. Sci., December, 1900. (389)

As might naturally have been expect-ed, the greater number of the species represented in the present collection are such as occur over the more northern portion of this Continent, not extending farther southward than the mountains of New Hampshire and Colorado. Besides the new genus *Ornithodes,* which be-longs to the family Tipulidae, the most

in ge____ ____ ___ Chi-ror ____ ____lore known only from St. Paul Island, in the Indian Ocean.

Family MYCETOPHILID. Diadocldia borealis sp. nov.

Head and antennae dark brown, two basal joints of the latter, also the pro-boscis and palpi, yellow, thorax pol-ished, yellow, the dorsum, except the front corners, dark brown, scutellum yellow, metanotum brown; abdomen dark brown, slightly polished, its hairs yellowish; coxaa and femora light yel-low, tibiae and tarsi brown, front tarsi slender; knob of halteres yellowish brown; wings hyaline, densely covered with short hairs, auxiliary crossvein pre-sent, tip of first vein about opposite apex of anterior branch of the fifth. Length 4 mm. A male specimen, col-lected June 3.

Habitat.—Lowe Inlet, British Colum-bia. *Type.*—Cat. no. 5190, U. S. Nation-al Museum.

Closely related to the European *D. fer-ruginosa* Meigen, of which species the U. S. National Museum contains two specimens from the White Mountains, New Hampshire; but in that species the apex of the first vein is far before the tip of the anterior branch of the fifth, the auxiliary crossvein is wanting, etc.

Hesperinus brevifrons Walker.

Hesperinus brevifrons Walker, List Dipt. Ins. British Museum, I, p. 8i, 1848.

Popof Island, Alaska: A single speci-men, collected July 8. This species was originally described from Hudson Bay, British America, and has been recorded from the mountains of New Hampshire and Colorado. The genus *Hesperinus* has heretofore been placed in the family Bibionidae, but it differs from all the other members of that family by the elongated antennae. In this and other structural characters it agrees very well with the members of the present family.

Necempheria kincaidi sp. nov.

Head and its members black, second

joint of antennae yellow, about one-half as long as the third, the three ocelli in a transverse row and widely separated from each other; thorax black, opaque, gray pruinose, the mesonotum marked with four polished vittae, scutellum black, the base narrowly yellow, its hairs and those of the thorax golden yellow; abdomen brownish black, slightly polished, its hairs yellowish; coxae and femora yellow, tibiae yellowish brown, tarsi dark brown, front tarsi toward their apices noticeably higher than wide; halteres yellow; wings hyaline, bare, auxiliary vein ending in the first before middle of inner submarginal cell, the latter about twice as long as wide, anterior fork of fourth vein about ten times as long as preceding section of this vein, fifth vein forking far before small crossvein, the latter shorter than first section of third vein. Length 6 mm. A female specimen, collected July 8. *Habitat.*—Popof Island, Alaska. *Type.*—Cat. no. 5191, U. S. National Museum.

Readily distinguished by its venation from any of the described species. Respectfully dedicated to Professor Trevor Kincaid, whose extensive captures have added so much to our knowledge of the fauna of this interesting region.

Anaclinia nemoralis Meigen.

Anaclinia nemoralis Meigen, System. Besch. Eur. Zweif. Ins., I, p. 265, 1818, Sitka, Alaska: Two specimens, collected June 16. A European species now for the first time reported from this country.

Boletina grcenlandica Staeger.

Boletina grcenlandica Staeger, Krqjer's Natur. Tidsskrift, p. 356, 1845.

Berg Bay, June 10; Yakutat, June 21; Virgin Bay, June 26; Orca, June 27; Popof Island, Alaska, July 12: Six specimens. Originally described from Greenland. Specimens are in the U. S. National Museum from the mountains of New Hampshire and Colorado.

Boletina inops sp. nov.

Black, the second joint of antennae and base of the third, the palpi, halteres, coxa, femora, and male hypopygium yellow, tibiae brownish yellow; hairs of body yellow; thorax subopaque, thinly gray pruinose; abdomen subopaque;

bristles of inner side of middle tibiae slightly shorter than the diameter of each tibia; wings hyaline, tip of auxiliary vein slightly before base of third vein, no auxiliary crossvein, fourth vein forking slightly beyond, the fifth about opposite to, base of third vein; third joint of antennae twice as long as wide, hypopygium of male at least one-half longer than the longest segment of the abdomen preceding it. Length 4.5 mm. A specimen of each sex, taken June 21 and 27.

Habitat.—Yakutat and Orca, Alaska. *Type.*—Cat. no. 5192, U. S. National Museum.

Readily recognized among the black forms by the unspotted wings, which have no indication of an auxiliary crossvein. Sciara abbreviate Walker.

Sciara abbreviata Walker, List Dipt. Ins. British Museum, 1, p. 109, 1848.

Popof Island, Alaska: Three females, collected June 12, 14, and 16. Originally described from Hudson Bay, British America. Sciara grcenlandlca Holmgren.

Sciara grcenlandica Holmgren, Ofversigt Vet.-Akad. Forhand., p. 104, 1872.

Popof Island, Alaska: Three females, collected July 10. Heretofore reported only from Greenland. Sciara iridipennis Zetterstedt.

Sciara iridipennis Zetterstedt, Insecta Lapp., p. 827, 1840.

Popof Island, July 12 and 15; Muir Inlet, Alaska, June 12: Eight specimens. Originally described from Lappland, and also reported from Greenland. Sciara borealis Riibsaamen.

Sciara borealis Rubsaamen, Bibliotheca Zool., p. 109, 1898.

Sitka, Alaska: Two specimens, collected June 16. Originally described from Greenland. Sciara tridentata Riibsaamen.

Sciara tridentata Rubsaamen, Bibliotheca Zool., p. 107, 1898.

Lowe Inlet, British Columbia: A single specimen, collected June 3. It was originally described from Greenland. Sciara expolita sp. nov.

Head black, mouth parts and antennae blackish brown, third joint of antennae almost twice as long as broad, the

eighth joint the same, its upper and lower edges parallel; thorax black, mesonotum highly polished, humeri pale yellow, prolonged as a triangular spot on the pleura; scutellum and metanotum black, the latter highly polished; abdomen pale yellow, the sides, hind margin of the segments, also the apical portion of the abdomen beyond the sixth segment, black, the end lamella slightly longer than broad; coxae and femora pale yellow, tibiae brownish yellow, tarsi brown; halteres dark brown, base of the peduncle yellow; wings grayish hyaline, last section of first vein distinctly longer than the preceding section, apex of first vein noticeably beyond the forking of the fourth, lower fork of the fourth vein considerably shorter than the preceding section of this vein. Length 4 mm. A female specimen, collected June 16. *Habitat.*—Sitka, Alaska.

Type.—Cat. no. 5193, U. S. National Museum.

Family SIMULHD.ffi. Simulium ochraceum Walker.

Simulium ochraceum Walker, Trans. Ent. Soc. London, p. 332, 1861.

Lowe Inlet, British Columbia, June 6; Sitka, Alaska, June 16; Virgin Bay, June 26; Kukak Bay, Alaska Peninsula, July 4: Ten specimens. Originally described from Mexico. The U. S. National Museum contains specimens collected in the mountains of Colorado and Montana.

Simulium invenustum Walker.

Simulium invenustum Walker, List Dipt. Ins. Brit. Mus., I, p. 112, 1848. *Simulium pecuarum* Riley, Report U. S. Dept. Agric., p. 512, 1886.

Metlakahtla, June 4; Sitka, June 16; Yakutat, June 21; Virgin Bay, June 26; Kukak Bay, July 4; Popof Island, July 8, 10, 11 and 16; Kadiak, Alaska, July 20: Twelve specimens. Originally described from Hudson Bay, British America. In the United States its known range extends from New Hampshire southward to Mississippi, and westward to Colorado.

Simulium venustum Say.

Simulium venustum Say, Jour. Acad. Nat. Sciences, Philadelphia, p. 28,

1823. *Simulium molestum* Harris, Insects Inj. Vegetation, 3d edit., p. 601, 1862. *Simulium piscicidium* Riley, Amer. Entomologist, 11, p. 367, 1870. Metlakahtla, June 4; Kukak Bay, July 4; Popof Island, July 8 to 11: Twelve specimens. The type locality of this species is given by

Say as "Shippingport, Falls of the Ohio." Shippingport is the old landing on the Kentucky side below the Falls of the Ohio. Its site is covered by the present city of Louisville, Kentucky. This species occurs all over the United States, as well as in Canada and British Columbia.

Simulium vittatum Zetterstedt.

Simulium vittatum Zetterstedt, Insecta Lapponica, p. 803, 1840. *Simulium argus* Williston, North American Fauna, No. 7, p. 253, 1893.

Yakutat, June 21; Kadiak, Alaska, July 20: Twelve specimens

A European species which is also reported as occurring in Greenland. It ranges over the northern portion of the United States, extending as far southward as New Jersey, Kansas, and southern California.

Family BIBIONUXffi.

Bibio variabilis Loew.

Bibio variabilis Loew, Berliner En torn. Zeitsch., p. 53, 1864.

Lowe Inlet, British Columbia, June 3; Metlakahtla, June 4; Berg Bay, June 10; Muir Inlet, June 12; Sitka, June 16; Yakutat, Alaska, June 21: Twenty-two males and eight females. Loew's original specimens came from Sitka and from New Hampshire. The species also occurs in Oregon.

Bibio obscurus Loew.

Bibio obscurus Loew, Berliner Entom. Zeitsch., p. 52, 1864.

Yakutat, June 21; Saldovia, Alaska, July 21: Four males and one female. This species was originally described from the vicinity of Hudson Bay, British America.

Dilophus serraticollis Walker.

Dilophus serraticollis 'W'alker, List Dipt. Ins. Brit. Museum, I, p. 117, 1848.

Metlakahtla, June 4; Berg Bay, June 10; Muir Inlet, June 12; Sitka, June 16; Yakutat, June 21; Virgin Bay, June 26;

Kukak Bay, July 4; Popof Island, July 12; Saldovia, July 21; Juneau, Alaska, July 26: Twenty-two males and thirty-four females. Originally described from Hudson Bay, but also occurs in Canada and Colorado.

Scatopse notata Linne.

Scatopse notata Linne, Fauna Suecica, p. 1773, 1761.

Popof Island, July 8 and 10; Juneau, Alaska, July 28: Eight specimens. A European species, which has also been reported as occuring in Greenland. It ranges as far southward at least as Alabama.,

Family CULICID-E.

Culei impiger Walker.

Culex impiger Walker, List Dipt. Ins. Brit. Museum, I, p. 6, 1848.

Sitka, June 16; Yakutat, June 21; Virgin Bay, June 26; Popof Island, Alaska, July 8 to 16: Fifty female specimens. This species was originally described for the vicinity of Hudson Bay, British America, and ranges southward to Jamaica, West Indies.

Culex consobrinus Desvoidy.

Culex consobrinus Desvoidy, Memoirs Soc. Hist. Nat. Paris, p. 408, 1827.

Sitka, June 16; Yakutat, Alaska, June 21: Three female specimens. Originally described from Pennsylvania; at the east it does not appear to occur south of the State mentioned, but ranges northward into British America. West of the Mississippi, however, it ranges southward to Nebraska, New Mexico, and southern California.

Family CHIRONOMHXE. Telmatogeton alaskensis sp. nov.

Head and its members brownish black, the front velvet black, first joint of antennae velvet brown; antennae about as long as the head, the first joint nearly three times as wide as the others, the latter subcylindrical, the last joint slightly wider than the others and subconical in profile; thorax opaque, black, the lateral margins and upper part of pleura varied with yellowish; scutellum, metonotum, and abdomen brownish black, the lateral margins of the latter and hind margins of the ventral segments, yellow; coxae mottled black, brown and yellowish, remainder of legs

blackish brown, front femora each bearing a transverse, contiguous pair of blunt tubercles near the tip of the under side, and just beyond them a pair of rather widely separated cavities; front tibiae each bearing a blunt tubercle on the under side near the base, the inner side of each front tibia rather strongly dilated at its first third; first joint of the tarsi nearly three times as long as the second, each of the last three joints slightly over one-half as long as the second joint, claws cleft almost to the middle; halteres whitish; wings brownish gray, veins brown, first section of the fourth vein yellow, third vein on its basal portion almost touching the first; length 4.5 mm. Four male specimens, collected June 21.

Habitat.—Yakutat, Alaska. *Type.*—Cat. no. 5194, U. S. National Museum.

The present genus, which is new to our fauna, was founded on a species inhabiting St. Paul Island, in the southern part of the Indian Ocean. Our species agrees very well with Dr. Schiner's description and figures except in the structure of the legs, but these are not sufficiently different to warrant the establishing of a separate genus for the present form.

Chasmatonotus univittatus sp. nov.

Black, the bases of antennae, front corners and hind end of thorax, pleura, except the lower portion and one or two spots; halteres, trochanters, and bases of femora and of tibiae, yellow; posterior margins of abdominal segments whitish; mesonotum polished; abdomen subopaque; wings black, the extreme base and a vitta extending from it three-fourths the length of the wing, between the fourth and fifth veins, white; length 2.5 mm. Five male specimens, collected June 16. -*Habitat.*—Sitka, Alaska.

Type.—Cat. no. 5195, U. S. National Museum. Readily distinguished from our other two species by the coloring of the wings.

Eutanypus borealis Coquillett.

Eutanypus borealis Coquillett, The Fur-seals and Fur-seal Islands N Pacific, iv, p. 341, 1899.

Muir Inlet, Alaska: A single specimen, collected June 12. This species, was originally described from the Bering Islands, but also occurs in New Mexico and New Hampshire.

Ceratopogon arcticus sp. nov.

Black, the knobs of the halteres and hairs on apical portion of antenna of male, and entire antennae of female, whitish; thorax polished, the abdomen opaque; femora slender, destitute of spinous bristles, first tarsal joint at least twice as long as the second, the last joint not spinose below, claws minute and of an equal size; wings hyaline, bare, the third vein on its basal fourth united to the first vein, tip of the latter nearly opposite apex of first third of the third vein, apex of third vein at about three-fourths length of vving, petiole of second posterior cell slightly shorter than the small crossvein. Length 1 mm. One male and eleven females, collected July 8 to 16.

Habitat.—Popof Island, Alaska. Type.—Cat. no. 5196, U. S. National Museum.

Ceratopogon femoratus Fabricius.

Ceratopogon femoratus Fabricius, Systema Antliatorum, p. 45, 1805.— Winnertz, Linnaea Entom., p. 68, 1852.

Popof Island, Alaska: A male specimen, collected July 13. This European species has not heretofore been reported from our Continent.

Ceratopogon hirtulus sp. nov.

Dull black, the legs and halteres yellow, hairs mostly light colored; mesonotum subopaque, thinly dark grayish pruinose; abdomen somewhat polished; femora slender, destitute of spinous bristles, first joint of tarsi longer than the second, fifth joint not spinose below, claws minute and of an equal size; wings grayish hyaline, bare except a few scattered hairs in the apical portion, most numerous in the costo-apical half of the first posterior cell; third vein greatly dilated, united on at least its apical half with the first, its apex considerably beyond middle of wing, petiole of second posterior cell longer than the small crossvein. Length i mm. Two females, collected June 26.

Habitat.—Virgin Bay,-Prince William Sound, Alaska. Type.—Cat. no. 5197, U. S. National Museum.

Ceratopogon cilipes sp. nov.

Black, legs brown, knobs of halteres yellow, hairs mostly light colored, those on basal half of antennae black; mesonotum polished, the abdomen less so; femora rather robust, destitute of spinous bristles, front and middle tibiae outwardly ciliate with suberect, scale-like hairs, first two joints of hind tarsi subcqual in length, the last joint not spinose below, the claws small and of an equal size; wings wholly covered with hairs, hyaline, the costal cell brownish, third vein united to the first except for a short distance beyond its middle, its apex near middle of length of wing, petiole of second posterior cell shorter than the small crossvein. Length 1.5 mm. Two female specimens, collected June 12.

Habitat.—Muir Inlet, Glacier Bay, Alaska. Type.—Cat. no. 5198, U. S. National Museum.

Family PSYCHODIDE. Psychoda pacifica Kincaid.

Psychoda pacifica Kincaid, Entomological News, p. 143, 1897.

Lowe Inlet, British Columbia: Two specimens, collected June 3. Originally described from Washington, but also reported as extending from Alaska to northern California.

Pericoma bipunctata Kincaid.

Pericoma bipunctata Kincaid, Entomological News, p. 34, 1899.

Berg Bay, June 10; Yakutat, Alaska, June 21: Thirteen specimens. Originally described from Washington and California. This and the preceding species were identified by Mr. Kincaid, from a comparison with the type specimens.

Family TTPULIIXffi. Dicranomyia venusta Bergroth.

Dicranomyia venusta Bergroth, Wiener Entom. Zeitung, p. 193, 1888.

Yakutat, Alaska: A single specimen, collected June 21. This species was originally described from Alaska.

Dicranomyia halterata Osten Sacken.

Dicranomyia halterata Osten Sacken, Monographs Diptera N. Am., iv, p. 71, 1869.

Muir Inlet, June 12; Popof Island, Alaska, July 10 and 16: Eight specimens. Originally described from Labrador, and Bergroth has already reported it

from Alaska.

Dicranomyia infuscata Doane.

Dicranomyia infuscata Doane, Journal N. Y. Ent. Soc., Sept., p. 185, 1900.

Yakutat, Alaska: A male specimen, collected June 21. Originally described from Collins, Idaho.

Limnobia sciopbila Osten Sacken.

Limnobia sciophila Osten Sacken, Bulletin U. S. Geol. Geog. Survey Terr., i11, p. 197, 1877.

Kadiak, July 20; Saldovia, Alaska, July 21: Three specimens. Originally described from northern California, but also occurs in Colorado.

Rhypholophus affinis Lundbeck.

Rhypholophus affinis Lundbeck, Videnskabelige Med. Nat. For. Kjob., p. 266, 1898.

Lowe Inlet, British Columbia: A male specimen, collected June 3. Originally described from Greenland.

Rhypholophus flaveolus sp. nov.

Yellow, the upper side of occiput and posterior part of the front black, gray pruinose, the antennae and palpi, except first joint of each, also the legs, except the coxa, trochanters, and bases of femora, dark brown; hairs of body nearly wholly yellow; antennae reaching slightly beyond insertion of wings, tapering to the apex, the joints beyond the second somewhat elliptical, scarcely longer than broad, the hairs less than twice as long as greatest diameter of the joints from which they spring; wings grayish hyaline, wholly covered with hairs, veins yellow, stigma scarcely apparent, discal cell opening into the second posterior, seventh vein toward its apex strongly diverging from the sixth. Length 4 mm. A male specimen, collected June 27.

Habitat.—Orca, Alaska. Type.—Cat. no. 5200, U. S. National Museum. Related to holotrichus, but of a much lighter color and with the anal cell greatly dilated at its apex.

Molophilus colonus Bergroth.

Molophilus colonus Bergroth, Wiener Entom. Zeitung, p. 195, 1888.

Virgin Bay, Alaska: A male specimen, collected June 26. This species was originally described from Alaska.

Molophilus falcatus Bergroth.

Molophilus faleatus Bergroth, Wiener Entom. Zeitung, p. 196, 1888.
Metlakahtla, June 4; Yakutat, Alaska, June 21: Two males and two females. Originally described from Alaska.

Molophilus paulus Bergroth.
Molophilus paulus Bergroth, Wiener Entom. Zeitung, p. 196, 1888.
Metlakahtla, June 4; Sitka, June 16; Popof Island, July 9; Kadiak, Alaska, July 20: Two males and two females. Originally described from Alaska.

Helobia hybrida (Meigen).
Limonia hybrida Meigen, Klass. Besch. Eur. Zwief. Ins., p. 57, 1804. *Limnobi-apunctipennis* Meigen, Sys. Besch. Eur. Zweif. Ins., 1, p. 147, 1818. *Symplecta punctipennis* Osten Sacken, Monographs Diptera N. Amer., IV, p. 171, 1869.
Saldovia, Alaska: A female specimen, collected July 21. This European species occurs over the greater portion of the United States.

Limnophila unica Osten Sacken.
Limnophila unica Osten Sacken, Monographs Diptera N. Amer., iv, p. 205, 1869.
Sitka, June 16; Yakutat, Alaska, June 21: Two male specimens. Originally described from New Hampshire.

Limnophila indistincta Doane.
Limnophila indistincta Doane, Journal K. Y. Ent. Soc., Sept., p. 191, 1900.
Yakutat, Alaska: A male specimen, collected June 21. This species was originally described from Collins, Idaho.

Tricyphona vitripennis (Doane).
Amalopis vitripennis Doane, Journal N. Y. Ent. Soc., Sept., p. 195, 1900.
Lowe Inlet, British Columbia: Two male specimens, collected June 3. Originally described from Washington.

Tricyphona disphana (Doane).
Amalopis disphana Doane, Journal N. Y. Ent. Soc., Sept., p. 195, 1900.
Yakutat, June 10; Berg Bay, June 21; Popof Island, Alaska, July 15: Three male specimens. Also originally described from Washington.

Ornithodes gen. nov.
Near *Tricyphona,* but the rostrum about one and a-half times as long as the head; palpi inserted near apex of the rostrum, eyes densely pubescent, head prolonged backward in the form of a rather long neck, prothorax considerably prolonged forward, antennae sixteen-jointed, tibiae with large spurs at their apices, tarsal claws simple, empodia narrow but rather long; apex of auxiliary vein opposite base of fourth posterior cell, auxiliary crossvein at more than twice the length of the hind crossvein before base of second vein, the latter slightly before the apex of seventh vein; second vein simple, the third issuing from it slightly before the small crossvein and forking a short distance beyond the latter; five posterior cells, the second petiolate.
Type.—The following species: Ornithodes harrimani sp. nov.

Black, the halteres, posterior margins of the abdominal segments except the first, apices of coxae, trochanters, and bases of femora yellow; antennae nearly reaching insertion of wings, slightly tapering to the apex, bearing a few short bristly hairs, first joint about twice as long as broad, the remaining joints except the last one about as long as broad or only slightly longer; head and thorax opaque, gray pruinose, mesonotum marked with four black vittae; abdomen slightly polished, its sparse hairs yellowish, claspers transverse oval, one and a-half times as broad as long, destitute of processes, posterior ventral margin of the preceding segment prolonged in the middle in the form of two large tubercles; wings hyaline, veins brownish, stigma pale grayish, a brown cloud at base of second vein, at apex of auxiliary vein, on marginal crossvein, on veins at bases of both submarginal, first, third, fourth, and fifth posterior cells, and beyond middle of second submarginal cell; base of first posterior cell directly above base of discal, hind crossvein about half its length before base of discal cell and more than its length before base of fourth posterior cell, discal cell closed. Length, including the rostrum, 15 mm. A male specimen, collected June 22.
Habitat.—Virgin Bay, Prince William Sound, Alaska. *Type.*—Cat. no. 5203, U. S. National Museum.
Respectfully dedicated to Mr. Edward H. Harriman, to whose generosity we are indebted for the discovery of this and many other interesting forms of insect life.

Pedicia obtusa Osten Sacken.
Pedicia obtusa Osten Sacken, Bulletin U. S. Geol. Geog. Survey Terr., i11, p. 205, 1877.—Aldrich, Psyche, p. 202, 1895.
Kadiak, Alaska: A male specimen, collected July 20. Originally described from northern California, and Professor Aldrich has reported its occurrence in northern Washington.

Dicranota argentea Doane.
Dicranota argentea Doane, Journal N. Y. Ent. Soc., Sept., p". 196, 1900.
Berg Bay, Alaska: A male specimen, collected June 10. The type locality of this species is Seattle, Wash.

Rhapbidolabis debilis Williston.
Rhaphidolabis Williston, Kansas Univ. Quart., p. 62, 1893.
Sitka, June 16; Yakutat, June 21; Virgin Bay, June 26; Saldovia, Alaska, July 21: Eight specimens. Originally described from California.

Cylindrotoma juncta sp. nov.
Head yellow, the middle of the front and the occiput, except next the eyes, dark brown, somewhat polished, upper side of rostrum, the palpi and antennae also brown; antennae reaching middle of third abdominal segment, the first two joints broader than long, the others cylindrical, each, except the last one, almost four times as long as broad; thorax yellowish, mesonotum masked with three opaque black vittae and with a narrow, curved, polished, brown stripe passing in front of them and extending below each of the outer ones, finally uniting with them at their apices; prothorax, except its hind margin, brown, a brown spot near center of pleura, a second below it between the front and middle coxae, and a brown vitta in front of the halteres; scutellum and lower median part of metanotum brown; abdomen brown, slightly polished, claspers yellow at their apices, destitute of processes, the median yellow, polished projection three-pronged; legs yellow, bases of coxae and apices of tarsi black; halteres yellow, the knobs brown; wings

hyaline, costal cell pale gray, stigma brownish gray, base of submarginal cell far beyond base of discal, five posterior cells, base of the second slightly before base of third. Length 10 mm. A male specimen, collected June 26.

Habitat.—Virgin Bay, Prince William Sound, Alaska. *Type.*—Cat. no. 5204, U. S. National Museum.

Closely related to *distinctissima* Meigen, of Europe, but the coloring is different and the male claspers are unarmed.

Tipula septentrionalis Loew.

Tipula septentrionalis Loew, Berliner Ent. Zeitsch., p. 278, 1863.

Virgin Bay, June 26; Kukak Bay, July 4; Popof Island, July 10; Kadiak, Alaska, July 20: Two males and three females; one of the females from Popof Island has aborted wings which are shorter than the thorax. Originally described from Labrador; the U. S. National Museum contains a male specimen, collected on Mount Washington, New Hampshire, by Mrs. Annie T. Slosson.

Tipula macrolabis Loew.

Tipula macrolabis Loew, Berliner Ent. Zeitsch., p. 58, 1864.

Saldovia, Alaska: A male specimen, collected July 21. This species was originally described from the region about Hudson Bay, British America, and a male specimen collected in the White Mountains, New Hampshire, is contained in the collection of the U. S. National Museum.

Tipula fallax Loew.

Tipula fallax Loew, Berliner Ent. Zeitsch., p. 281, 1863.

Sitka, June 16; Virgin Bay, June 21; Kukak Bay, July 1 and 4; Kadiak, Alaska, July 20: Two males and six females. Originally described from California.

Tipula appendiculata Loew.

Tipula appendiculata Loew, Berliner Ent. Zeitsch., p. 287, 1863.

Popof Island, July 10; Kadiak, July 20; Juneau, Alaska, July 25: Nine males and seven females. Originally described from the Saskatchewan River, British America.

Tipula besselsi Osten Sacken.

Tipula besselsi Osten Sacken, Proc. Boston Soc. Nat. Hist., p. 42, 1876.

Muir Inlet, Alaska: Three males and one female, collected June 12. The type locality of this species is Grinnel Land, British America, latitude 82 north.

Tipula strigata sp. nov.

Front and occiput black, gray pruinose, marked with a median black vitta; rostrum varying from brown to yellow, palpi brown, antennae black, the first two joints and base of the third, yellow; antennae of male, if stretched backward, would reach base of third abdominal segment, slightly tapering toward the apex, third joint the longest, slightly thickening at its apex, bearing several irregularly arranged bristles on its basal two-thirds; remaining joints becoming successively slightly shorter, each slightly constricted near the middle, bearing a whorl of bristles near the base, the seventh joint over three times as long as wide; antennae of female almost reaching base of wing, considerably tapering to the apex, formed as in the male except that the joints beyond the fifth are not constricted in the middle, the seventh joint less than twice as long as wide; thorax bare, black, opaque, gray pruinose, a yellow vitta extending from below each humerus to root of wing and from thence to the scutellum, sending a branch downward behind the front coxa; the three usual vittae are concolorous with the mesonotum, each margined with black, the two black lines bordering the median vitta straight, anteriorly diverging, their anterior ends widely separated, a brown vitta midway between them, which is sometimes almost obsolete; scutellum brown, gray pruinose, its margin and lower side yellow; metanotum black, gray pruinose, the sides spotted with yellow; abdomen bare, yellow, a black vitta on each side of the middle; male hypopygium large, black, the apex and under side yellow, ventral portion of the preceding (eighth) abdominal segment bearing sparse, short, black hairs; claspers almost square, each bearing near the apex of the inner side a pair of spatulate organs which are about as long as the clasper, the upper pair converging, the lower one curving outward;

dorsal piece of hypopygium at middle of its posterior margin bearing a pair of conical, blunt-pointed, backwardly projecting processes which are more than one-half as long as the dorsal piece; ovipositor black at its base, the remainder yellow, nearly as long as the second abdominal segment, the upper pair of sheaths tapering to their middle, then of nearly an equal width, not crenulate, the apex bluntly rounded; wings pale grayish, costal cell yellowish, auxiliary vein yellow, the others brown, stigma brown, a white spot before its base, a less distinct one beyond its apex and a similar one in base of discal cell, this cell more than twice as long as wide; legs yellow, apices of femora and of tibiae black, tarsi changing into black at its apex; halteres brown, the bases yellow. Length of male, 14 mm.; of female, 18 mm. Two males and one female.

Habitat.—Metlakahtla, June 4; Sitka, June 16; Yakutat, Alaska, June 21. *Type.*—Cat. no. 5205, U. S. National Museum. Tipula tenebrosa sp. nov.

Same as the above description of *strigata* with these exceptions: Front and occiput destitute of a median black vitta, rostrum brown, the under side yellow, third joint of antennae wholly black, antennae of male not reaching beyond base of abdomen, the third joint bearing a few scattered bristles, seventh antennal joint of female nearly three times as long as broad; thorax bearing many rather short whitish hairs on its dorsum, scutellum wholly black, yellow spots on sides of metanotum small or wanting; abdomen thinly covered with short, pale yellowish hairs, black, the venter, at least basally, and sometimes the hind margins of some of the segments, yellow; ventral portion of eighth abdominal segment bearing many pale yellowish hairs, claspers nearly twice as long as wide, the lower outer angle considerably prolonged beyond the upper one, each clasper bearing near the apex of the inner side a pair of flattened processes, the anterior one nearly oval, the other subconical, its apex furnished with a brown, corneous tooth; upper pair of sheaths of ovipositor tapering for three-fourths of their length; discal cell less than twice as long as wide; femora and tibiae of female yellow, in the male brown with bases of femora yellow. Length of male, 12 mm.; of female, 15 mm. A specimen of each sex.

Habitat.—Berg Bay, June 10; Muir Inlet, Alaska, June 11.

Type.—Cat. no. 5206, U. S. National Museum.

Tipula gelida sp. nov.

Differs from the description of the male of *strigata* only as follows: Front and occiput destitute of a median black vitta, rostrum black, third joint of antennae wholly black, antennae not reaching base of abdomen, the third joint slightly more than twice as long as wide; the three mesonotal vittae are black, the median one divided in the middle by a gray line; scutellum and metanotum not marked with yellow; abdomen black, opaque, gray pruinose, the hind margins of the segments, except the first, and a lateral vitta, yellow, sparsely covered with very short yellowish hairs; hypopygium small, black, gray pruinose, ventral portion of eighth abdominal segment sparsely yellowish pubescent, claspers nearly orbicular, each bearing near the apex of the inner side an oval, inwardly curving process which is nearly as long as the clasper; dorsal piece of the hypopygium destitute of processes on its hind margin; whitish spots of wings indistinct, discal cell less than twice as long as broad. Length 14 mm. Six male specimens captured June 4.

Habitat.—Metlakahtla, Alaska. *Type.*—Cat. no. 5207, U. S. National Museum.

Tipula cineracea sp. nov.

Equals the description of *strigata* with these exceptions: Antennal joints four to eleven in the male strongly constricted in the middle, the seventh about two and one-half times as long as its greatest width; antennae of female reaching middle of metanotum, slightly tapering to the apex; of the usual three mesonotal vittae, the outer ones are wholly wanting, the median one is gray, bordered with a pair of black lines and with a third black line midway between them; abdomen sparsely covered with very short yellowish hairs, yellow, marked with a median black vitta which is usually almost obsolete on base of abdomen and in the male is broadly expanded posteriorly, male hypopygium rather small, yellow, ventral portion of the eighth abdominal segment bearing a few short, yellowish hairs; claspers transversely oval, the upper of the two processes near apex of inner side of each is somewhat clavate, slightly longer than the clasper, the other is about twice as long as this one and about four times as broad, with two large grooves on the outer side toward its apex strongly curving upward, the apex dark brown and terminating in a flattened, rather narrow process in front of the base of which is a large brown lobe; dorsal piece of hypopygium destitute of processes; ovipositor yellow, noticeably longer than the second abdominal segment; white spots of wings indistinct, discal cell only slightly longer than broad. Length of male, 11 to 13 mm.; of female, 15 to 19 mm. Seventeen males and six females.

Habitat.—Yakutat, June 21; Kukak Bay, Alaska Peninsula, July 4; Popof Island, July 10; Kadiak, Alaska, July 20.

Type.—Cat. no. 5208, U. S. National Museum.

The U. S. National Museum contains a female specimen of this species collected at Fort Wrangell, Alaska, by Professor H. F. Wickham.

Tipula spernax Osten Sacken.

Tipula spernax Osten Sacken, Bulletin U. S. Geol. Geog. Survey Terr., iii, p. 210, 1877.

Metlakahtla, Alaska: A male specimen, collected June 4. This species was originally described from the mountains of California.

Pachyrrhina vittula Loew.

Pachyrrhina vittula Loew, Berliner Ent. Zeitsch., p. 63, 1864.

Muir Inlet, Alaska: Two male specimens, collected June 12. The original habitat is the vicinity of Hudson Bay, British America.

Proc. Wash. Acad. Sci., November, 1900.

Family XYLOPHAGID.E. Leptis dimidiate Loew.

Leptis dimidiata Loew, Berliner Ent. Zeitsch., p. 10, 1863.

Juneau, Alaska: Three specimens, collected July 26. This species was originally described from Alaska.

Leptis pruinosa Bigot.

Leptis pruinosa Bigot, Bulletin Soc. Zool. France, p. 19, 1887.

Popof Island, Alaska: Two specimens, collected July 10. Originally reported from Mount Hood, Oregon.

Symphoromyia pullate Coquillett.

Symphoromyia pullata Coquillett, Journal New York Ent. Soc., p. 56, 1894.

Sitka, Alaska: A male specimen, captured June 11. This species was originally described from Colorado and New Hampshire.

Spania edete Walker.

Spania edeta Walker, List Dipt. Ins. Brit. Museum, 111, p. 489, 1849.

Muir Inlet, June 12; Sitka, Alaska, June 16: Four specimens. Originally described from the Albany River, British America. Specimens are in the U. S. National Museum from the White Mountains, New Hampshire.

Family STRATIOMYIHXE. Beris annulifera (Bigot).

Op'acantha annulifera Bigot, Annates Soc. Ent. France, p. 21, 1887.

Sitka, June 16; Kukak Bay, July 4; Popof Island, Alaska, July 12: Four specimens. The type locality of this species is stated to be Georgia, but this may be erroneous. Specimens are in the U. S. National Museum from New Hampshire and Colorado.

Family TABANnXE. Chrysops nigripes Zetterstedt.

Chrysops nigripes Zetterstedt, Insecta Lapponica Descripta, p. 519, 1840.

Kukak Bay, Alaska: A female specimen, collected July 4. Originally described from Lapland, but Dr. Loew has also reported its occurrence in Alaska.

Tabanus septentrionalis Loew.

Tabanus septentrionalis Loew, Verh. Zool.-Bot. Gesell. Wien, p. 593, 1858.

Kukak Bay, July 4; Kadiak, Alaska, July 20: Seven specimens. This species was originally described from Labrador, and Osten Sacken has already reported its occurrence in Alaska.

Tabanus sonomensis Osten Sacken.

Tabanus sonomensis Osten Sacken, Bulletin U. S. Geol. Geog. Survey Terr.

, in, p. 216, 1877.

Fox Point, Alaska: Three specimens, captured July 28. Originally described from northern California.

Tabanus insuetus Osten Sacken.

Tabanus insuetus Osten Sacken, Bulletin U. S. Geol. Geog. Survey Terr., m, p. 219, 1877.

Virgin Bay, June 26; Juneau, July 26; Fox Point, Alaska, July 28: Three specimens. Also originally described from northern California.

Family Therevtdje. Thereva melanoneura Loew.

Thereva melanoneura Loew, Berliner Ent. Zeitsch., p. 250, 1872.

Kukak Bay, Alaska: Ten specimens, taken July 4. Originally described from California.

Family EMPIDUXffi.

Empis poplitea Loew.

Empispoplitea Loew, Berliner Ent. Zeitsch., p. 16, 1863.

Sitka, June 16; Yakutat, June 21; Kukak Bay, July 4; Kadiak, Alaska, July 20: Thirty-three specimens. Originally described from Alaska. Specimens are in the U. S. National Museum from Colorado.

Empis clauda sp. nov.

Black, the palpi, proboscis, humeri, lateral margins of metanotum, scutellum, a large spot below insertion of each wing, the halteres, coxae, and remainder of legs, also base of venter, yellow, apices of tarsi brown; eyes of male separated less than width of lowest ocellus, third joint of antennae broad at base, tapering rapidly to the apex, about twice as long as the style, proboscis slightly over twice as long as height of head; hairs and bristles of body and legs black; mesonotum opaque, gray pruinose, marked with four, indistinct, brownish vittae; scutellum bearing four bristles; abdomen slightly polished, hypopygium small, ascending obliquely, the dorsal piece prolonged at each posterior corner in the form of a flattened, almost linear process, central filament unusually robust, arcuate, free except toward its apex; no ventral process in front of the hypopygium; hind femora of male each bearing a hook-like process on the under side a short dis-

tance before the apex, curved backward and covered with short hairs, while beyond it are two, bare, pimple-like swellings; on the inner side of the femora nearer its apex is a fringe of about five rather short spinous bristles; hind tibiae of male each bearing a bare, slightly arcuate process on the outer side near the base, while opposite it, on the inner side, is a low prominence beset with short bristly hairs; legs of female simple, not fringed with scales; wings grayish hyaline, stigma brown, veins brown, normal. Length 5 to 7 mm. Seventeen males and fourteen females.

Habitat.—Yakutat, June 21; Popof Island, July 8 to 12; Kadiak, Alaska, July 20. *Type.*—Cat. no. 5209, U. S. National Museum.

Empis laniventris Eschscholz.

Empis laniventris Eschscholz, Entomographien, 1, p. 113, 1823.

Popof Island, Alaska: Seventy-eight specimens, collected from July 10 to. 15. Originally described from Alaska.

Empis virgata Coquillett.

Empis virgata Coquillett, Proc. U. S. National Museum, p. 408, 1896.

Sitka, June 16; Yakutat, June 21; Saldovia, Alaska, July 21: Seventy specimens. This species was heretofore known only from Washington.

Empis pellucida sp. nov.

Black, the palpi and horny part of proboscis, except its base, yellow, halteres yellowish white, bases of tibiae sometimes reddish yellow; eyes of male more widely separated than the posterior ocelli; third joint of antennae rather broad, gradually tapering to the apex, about five times as long as the style, proboscis twice as long as height of head; hairs and bristles of body and legs black; mesonotum slightly polished, marked with a median, light gray pruinose vitta, the lateral margins and pleura gray pruinose; scutellum bearing four bristles; abdomen highly polished, hypopygium of male small, almost bare, obliquely ascending, destitute of elongate processes, central filament robust, rapidly tapering toward the apex, arcuate, free except its apex; hind margin of fifth abdominal segment ventrally fringed with spinous bristles, many of

which are as long as this segment; legs in both sexes simple, first joint of hind tarsi slightly thicker than that of the front ones, hind femora spinose on the under side; wings hyaline, veins dark brown, normal, stigma brown. Length 6 mm. Three males and two females.

Habitat.—Virgin Bay, Prince William Sound, June 26; Kukak Bay, July 4; Popof Island, Alaska, July 9 and 11. *Type.*—Cat. no. 5210, U. S. National Museum.

Closely related to *virgata,* but in that species the spinous bristles on the ventral portion of the fifth abdominal segment in the male are arranged in a round cluster and none of them exceed one-fourth of the length of this segment; both sexes have the mesonotum dark gray pruinose and marked with three distinct, polished black vittae.

Empis fumida sp. nov.

Differs from the above description of *pellucida* only as follows: Palpi and proboscis black, legs always wholly black, eyes of male less widely separated than width of lowest ocellus, mesonotum highly polished, not distinctly vittate, scutellum bearing six or more bristles, hypopygium of male quite thickly covered with hairs, the central filament hidden except sometimes its apical portion, wings pale brown, more yellowish at base and in costal cell. Length 7 mm. Six males and four females.

Habitat.—Metlakahtla, in June; Virgin Bay, June 26; Kukak Bay, Alaska, July 4. *Type.*—Cat. no. 5211, U. S. National useum.

Empis infumata sp. nov.

Same as *fumida* except that the palpi and horny portion of the proboscis are yellow, central filament of hypopygium of male free except at the apex, no fringe nor cluster of spinous bristles on ventral portion of the fifth or other abdominal segments, hind femora destitute of spinous bristles on the under side, at most with a few weak bristles on the apical fourth. Length 5 mm. One male and three females, collected July 8 to 11.

Habitat.—Popof Island, Alaska. *Type.*—Cat. no. 5212, U. S. National Museum.

Empis brachysoma sp. nov.

Black, the palpi, horny portion of proboscis, stems of halteres, femora, and tibiae yellow, front and hind femora in both sexes, and hind tibiae in the male, yellowish brown, coxae brown basally, changing into yellow at their apices, tarsi and knobs of halteres dark brown, apex of male abdomen marked with yellow; eyes of male contiguous, third joint of antennae rather broad at base, quite rapidly tapering to the apex, about twice as long as the style, proboscis twice as long as height of head; hairs and bristles of mesonotum black, hairs of pleura and abdomen white; thorax opaque, gray pruinose, mesonotum marked with four, slightly polished, black vittae, scute Hum bearing from four to six black bristles; abdomen of male polished black in middle of dorsum, the sides opaque, gray pruinose; in the female the dorsum of segments two to four, and all of abdomen beyond the fifth segment is polished black, remainder of abdomen opaque, gray pruinose; hypopygium of male rather small, obliquely ascending, claspers destitute of processes, dorsal piece with a broad emargination in its posterior end almost reaching its center, central filament hidden, venter destitute of processes and of spinous bristles; legs of male simple, femora destitute of bristles and long hairs, first joint of hind tarsi noticeably thicker than that of the front ones; legs of female ciliate with nearly erect scales on both sides of the hind femora and tibiae, middle femora and apical half of upper side of the front femora; wings unusually long and narrow, grayish hyaline, stigma and veins, except at base of wing, dark brown, venation normal. Length 7 mm. A specimen of each sex, collected July 21.

Habitat.—Saldovia, Kenai Peninsula, Alaska.

Type.—Cat. no. 5213, U. S. National Museum.

Empis triangula sp. nov.

Black, the halteres and legs dark brown, knees yellow, this color rarely extending over the greater portion of the femora and sometimes of the tibiae, venter of abdomen of female largely yellow; eyes of male contiguous, third joint of antennae nearly linear, at least five times as long as broad, the style scarcely perceptible; proboscis from one and a-half to twice as long as height of head; hairs and bristles of thorax and scutellum black; thorax somewhat polished, very thinly gray pruinose, not distinctly vittate, scutellum bearing ten marginal bristles; abdomen slightly polished, hypopygium of male rather large, obliquely ascending, the lower piece bearing a cluster of rather long, black bristles at its apex, filament hidden, venter of abdomen destitute of processes and of spinous bristles; legs simple, slender, almost bare; wings hyaline, veins and stigma brown, second submarginal cell somewhat triangular, pointed at its base, about one and one-half times as long as broad, discal cell subequal in length to last section of fourth vein, last section of fifth vein half as long as the preceding section. Length 2 to 3.5 mm. Eight males and eighteen females.

Habitat.—Lowe Inlet, British Columbia, June 3; Farragut Bay, June 8; Sitka, June 16; Yakutat, Alaska, June 21. *Type.*—Cat. no. 5214, U. S. National Museum.

Empis conjuncta sp. nov.

Differs from the above description of *triangula* only as follows: Legs and venter of abdomen dark brown, proboscis shorter than height of head, hypopygium of male wholly and sparsely covered with bristly hairs, destitute of a cluster of these hairs, the dorsal piece bearing a pair of long, subcylindrical, fleshy processes, which are covered with short hairs, filament free. Length 2. 5 mm. One male and two females.

Habitat.—Sitka, June 16; Orca, Alaska, June 27. *Type.*—Cat. no. 5215, U. S. National Museum.

Classified by its short proboscis, this species would be placed in the genus *Hilar a;* but its elongated third antennal joint with the minute style, the contiguous eyes of the male and the slender first joint of his front tarsi, indicate a nearer relationship with the typical species of the genus *Empis.*

Hilara aurata sp. nov.

Black, the first two antennal joints and the legs dark brown, the knees and halteres yellow; upper part of occiput and sides of front velvet black, middle of front below the lowest ocellus, face, cheeks, and lower part of occiput gray pruinose; eyes of male almost as widely separated as the posterior ocelli, third joint of antennae conical, slightly longer than broad, subequal in length to the style, proboscis as long as height of head, hairs of palpi and under side of head whitish, those of occiput yellowish brown; thorax slightly polished, marked with three indistinct black vittae, almost bare, in the middle, behind the suture, with a golden yellow pubescence, no hairs in front of the halteres, scute Hum bearing four bristles and a few short hairs; abdomen slightly polished, its hairs yellow, hypopygium of male small, nearly bare; legs destitute of long bristly hairs, first joint of front tarsi of male greatly swollen; wings hyaline, veins yellow, stigma pale yellowish, venation normal. Length 4 mm. A female specimen, colhected July 4. The U. S. National Museum contains a male specimen collected at Eastport, Maine, July 1, 1870, by Mr. Edward Burgess.

Habitat.—Kukak Bay, Alaska; Eastport, Maine. *Type.*—Cat. no. 5216, U. S. National Museum.

Hilara transfuga Walker.

Hilara transfuga Walker, List Dipt. Ins. Brit. Museum, i11, p. 491, 1849.
Berg Bay, June 10; Popof Island, Alaska, July 6 to 10: Ten specimens. Originally described from Albany River, British America.

Hilara quadrivittata Meigen.

Hilara quacirivittata Meigen, Syst. Besch. Eur. Zweif. Ins., I11, p. 7, 1822.
— Schiner, Fauna Austriaca, Diptera, I, p. 115.
Kukak Bay, July 4; Popof Island, July 8 to 10; Kadiak, Alaska, July 20: Twenty-eight specimens. This European species has not heretofore been reported from this Continent. The specimens agree perfectly with the descriptions above indicated.

Gloma obscura Loew.

Gloma obscura Loew, Berliner Ent.

Zeitsch., p. 84, 1864.

Yakutat, June 21; Virgin Bay, Alaska, June 26: Two specimens. Originally described from the White Mountains, New Hampshire.

Gloma scopifera sp. nov.

Black, a humeral dot, the halteres, second and third segments of abdomen, except middle of dorsum, under side of the fourth segment and the legs, yellow, the greater portion of the coxae, middle of femora, apices of tibiae, last two joints of front and middle tarsi, and whole of hind tarsi, except bases of first two joints, brown; all hairs and bristles black; third joint of antennae slightly longer than wide, less than half as long as the style; thorax somewhat opaque, thinly gray pruinose; abdomen slightly polished; front tibiae at apices bearing a dense cluster of rather long bristly hairs, last two joints of front tarsi greatly dilated and fringed along the sides with short bristly hairs, middle femora beyond the middle of the under side bearing a cluster of about three long bristles, middle tibia? swollen at middle of inner side, the swelling densely covered with short, bristly hairs; wings grayish hyaline, veins and stigma brown. Length 6 mm. Three male specimens, collected June 16.

Habitat.—Sitka, Alaska. Type.—Cat. no. 5217, U. S. National Museum. Cyrtoma pilipes Loew. Cyrtoma pilipes Loew, Berliner Ent. Zeitsch., p. 207, 1862.

Kukak Bay, July 4; Popof Island, Alaska, July 8 to 13: Twentyfive specimens. Originally described from Illinois.

Microphorus atratus sp. nov.

Black, including the hairs; eyes of male contiguous, third joint of antenna orbicular on its basal half, the remainder narrowed into a styliform process, style one and one-half times as long as the third antennal joint, proboscis less than half as long as height of head, body opaque, not pruinose, the hairs rather long, on the mesonotum abundant, on the abdomen sparse, scutellum bearing four bristles; under side of front and middle femora, both sides of the hind ones and outer side of the hind tibiae ciliate their entire length with rather

long hairs, first joint of hind tarsi noticeably thicker than that of either of the other tarsi, much narrower than the hind tibiae; wings hyaline, veins and stigma brown, venation normal, last section of fifth vein two-thirds as long as the preceding section, sixth vein obsolete beyond end of anal cell. Length 2 mm. A male specimen, collected July 20.

Habitat.—Kadiak, Alaska. Type.—Cat. no. 5218, U. S. National Museum.

Microphorus fiavipilosus sp. nov.

Black, the hairs, stems of halteres, femora and tibiae, yellow, knobs of halteres and the tarsi brown; eyes of male contiguous, third joint of antennae sublanceolate, only slightly tapering to the apex, over four times as long as the style, proboscis noticeably shorter than height of head, mesonotum highly polished, scutellum bearing about ten marginal bristles, abdomen slightly polished, hairs of legs sparse and rather short, first joint of hind tarsi slightly thicker than that of any of the other tarsi; wings hyaline, stigma smoky brown, veins yellowish brown, last section of fifth vein one-fourth as long as the preceding section, sith vein reaching almost to the wing margin; length 2 mm. Two male specimens, collected June 3.

Habitat.—Lowe Inlet, British Columbia. Type.—Cat. no. 5219, U. S. National Museum.

Microphorus crocatus sp. nov.

Yellow, the head and its members, a median vitta on mesonotum, dorsum of abdomen, and apices of tarsi dark brown, third joint of antennae sublanceolate, only slightly tapering to the apex, about twice as long as wide, five times as long as the style; proboscis about as long as height of head; hairs of body sparse and rather short, yellow; mesonotum polished, scutellum bearing about eight bristles, abdomen polished; hairs of legs very short, first joint of hind tarsi slightly thicker than that of any of the other tarsi; wings hyaline, veins yellowish brown, stigma almost obsolete, last section of fifth vein nearly half as long as the preceding section, sixth vein ending a short distance from the wing margin. Length 2 mm. A female specimen, collected June 26.

Habitat.—Sitka, Alaska. Type.—Cat. no. 5220, U. S. National Museum.

Rhamphomyia flavirostris Walker.

Rhamphomyia flavirostris Walker, List Dipt. Ins. Brit. Mus., i11, p. 501, 1849.

Muir Inlet, June 12; Popof Island, Alaska, July 10 and 12: Three specimens. Originally described from Albany River, British America.

Rhamphomyia corvina Loew.

Rhamphomyia corvina Loew, Berliner Ent. Zeitsch., p. 28, 1861.

Lowe Inlet, British Columbia, June 3; Kukak Bay, July 4; Juneau, Alaska, July 26: Three specimens. Originally described from New York. The U. S. National Museum contains specimens collected in Pennsylvania, District of Columbia, and North Carolina.

Rhamphomyia minytus Walker.

Rhamphomyia minytus Walker, List Dipt. Ins. Brit. Mus., i11, p. 502, 1849.

Berg Bay, June 10; Muir Inlet, June 11; Virgin Bay, Alaska, June 26: Six specimens. Originally described from Albany River, British America.

Rhamphomyia irregularis Loew.

Rhamphomyia irregularis Loew, Berliner Ent. Zeitsch., p. 81, 1864.

Kukak Bay, Alaska: A female specimen, taken July 4. Originally described from New Hampshire. The U. S. National Museum also contains specimens of both sexes collected in Colorado.

Rhamphomyia limbata Loew.

Rhamphomyia limbata Loew, Berliner Ent. Zeitsch., p. 32, 1861.

Sitka, June 16; Yakutat, June 21; Virgin Bay, June 26; Saldovia, Alaska, July 21: Eight female specimens. Originally reported from the District of Columbia. Specimens are contained in the U. S. National Museum collection from Illinois and Colorado.

Rhamphomyia villipes sp. nov.

Black, the halteres, hypopygium, femora, tibiae and tarsi yellow, apices of first four tarsal joints, and whole of the fifth, brown, coxae brown and yellow; eyes of male contiguous, third joint of antennae about four times as long as wide, two and one-half times as long as the style, proboscis twice as long as height of head; hairs of entire insect black; thorax opaque, gray pruinose, two indistinct brown subdorsal vittae, hairs abundant and rather long, scutellum bearing four bristles; abdomen opaque, densely whitish pruinose, thickly clothed with rather long hairs, hypopygium rather small, ascending, the claspers subhemispherical, thinly covered on the outer surface with rather long hairs, on the posterior portion bearing an oval, hairy process, near the middle of the inner side with a short, black, subcylindrical, hairy process, and at the apex bearing a long hairy process nearly as long as the clasper, of the shape of a half cylinder, the processes of the two claspers pressed together and having a circular opening near the apex of the upper side; filament appressed to the body of the hypopygium; front and hind sides of the front and middle tibiae and under side of the middle femora densely covered with rather long hairs, legs elsewhere more sparsely covered with similar hairs, middle femora distinctly arcuate; wings whitish hyaline, stigma pale brown, veins normal, yellow and brown, last section of fifth vein one and one-half times as long as the preceding section, sixth vein reaches the wing margin but is colorless from apex of anal cell two-thirds of distance to the wing margin. Length 10 mm. A male specimen, collected July 9.

Habitat.—Popof Island, Alaska. *Type.*—Cat. no. 5221, U. S. National Museum.

Closely related to *quinqttelineata,* but readily distinguished by the unusually hairy legs and processes on the hypopygium.

Rhamphomyia disparilis sp. nov.

Male: Black, the halteres yellowish; hairs of upper part of head, antennae, mesonotum, scutellum, several on the tibiae and many on the tarsi, black, remaining hairs yellowish; eyes separated more widely than the posterior ocelli, third joint of antennae slightly over twice as long as wide, three times as long as the style, proboscis slightly longer than height of head; mesonotum slightly polished, not distinctly vittate, its hairs short and sparse, scutellum bearing four bristles; abdomen polished, its hairs long and sparse, hypopygium

very large, porrect, lower outer angle of each clasper prolonged into a narrow, subconical process about as long as the basal portion, hypopygium bearing many very long bristly hairs, filament thread-like, the exposed portion fully seven times as long as the first joint of the hind tarsi, the latter and the second joint bearing many long hairs on their upper side, first joint of front tarsi as thick as the tibiae, much thicker than that of any of the other tarsi, middle tibiae on the outer side ciliate with a row of long bristly hairs; wings hyaline, veins and stigma brown, venation normal, last section of fifth vein nearly twice as long as the preceding section, sixth vein obliterated before reaching the wing margin. Length 3 to 4.5 mm.

Female: Differs from the male as follows: Anterior half of mesonotum opaque, gray pruinose, marked with four polished black vittae, the remainder of thorax, scutellum, and first five segments of abdomen, densely silvery white pruinose, hairs of abdomen rather short, hind tarsi and middle tibiae destitute of long, bristly hairs, first joint of front tarsi narrower than the tibiae, not so thick as that of the hind tarsi; discal cell prolonged almost to the wing margin, fourth vein not prolonged beyond its apex, no vein between second and third posterior cells, last section of fifth vein about one-sixth as long as the preceding section. Length 4 to 5 mm.

Five males and six females.

Habitat.—Yakutat, June 21; Virgin Bay, Alaska, June 26. *Type.*—Cat. no. 5222, U. S. National Museum.

Closely related to *limbata* and *irregularis,* but in those species the lower outer angle of the male claspers is rounded, and the fourth vein in both sexes is prolonged to the wing margin.

Rhamphomyia glauca sp. nov.

Black, the halteres light yellow, hairs and bristles black; eyes of male contiguous, third joint of antennae slightly over twice as long as wide, about four times as long as the style, proboscis about as long as height of head; body opaque, bluish gray pruinose, hairs sparse and rather short, scutellum bearing four bristles, hypopygium rather small,

obliquely ascending, bearing several long bristly hairs, claspers elongate conical, filament thread-like, the exposed portion about five times as long as first joint of hind tarsi, the latter much thicker than that of any of the other tarsi, much narrower than the tibiae, hind tibiae of male outwardly bearing several rather long bristly hairs, in the female ciliate with nearly erect scales, wings hyaline, stigma pale yellowish, veins yellowish brown, normal, last section of fifth vein over twice as long as the preceding section, sixth vein reaches the wing margin. Length 3 to 4 mm. A specimen of each sex.

Habitat.—Metlakahtla, June 4; Berg Bay, Alaska, June 10. *Type.*—Cat. no. 5223, U. S. National Museum.

Near *priapulus,* but in that species the sixth vein is obliterated before reaching the wing margin and the hind tibiae of the female are not ciliate with scales.

Rhamphomyia cineracea sp. nov.

Differs from the above description of *glauca* only as follows: Mesonotum slightly polished, thinly dark gray pruinose, hairs of male hypopygium sparse and rather short, the claspers suboval, near apex of under side bearing a dense cluster of rather short hairs, filament quite slender, the exposed portion only slightly longer than the first joint of the hind tarsi, hind tibiae of male outwardly bearing a few rather short bristles, in the female not ciliate with scales, last section of fifth vein sometimes less than twice as long as the preceding section. Length about 3 mm. Two males and five female?.

Habitat.—Sitka, June 16; Kukak Bay, July 4; Popof Island, July 8 to 10; Juneau, Alaska, July 26. *Type.*—Cat. no. 5224, U. S. National Museum.

More nearly related to *glauca* than to any of our other species.

Rhamphomyia limata sp. nov.

Differs from *glauca* as follow: Mesonotum marked with four polished vittae which sometimes almost meet each other; segments three to five of abdomen, and sides of the second, polished, the narrow hind margins of these segments whitish, hairs on-sides of abdomen rather abundant and long, claspers of male hypopygium somewhat oval, at the apex bearing a dense cluster of rather long hairs, filament robust, the exposed portion less than half as long as the first joint of the hind tarsi, hind tibiae of female not ciliate with scales, wings tinged with yellow, especially in the costal cell, stigma dark brown. Length 5 to 6 mm. One male and three females, collected June 8 and 9.

Habitat.—Popof Island, Alaska. *Type.* —Cat. no. 5225, U. S. National Museum.

Near *Jimbriata,* but in that species the mesonotum is marked with only three polished vittae, and the middle and hind femora of the female are ciliate on the under side with nearly erect scales.

Rhamphomyia barypoda sp. nov.

Differs from *glauca* as follows: Mesonotum slightly polished, thinly olive gray pruinose and marked with three indistinct black vittae; scutellum and abdomen polished, lower and posterior edges of male claspers thickly beset with rather long hairs, claspers nearly transversely trapezoidal, filament rather robust, sinuate, the exposed portion only slightly longer than the first joint of the hind tarsi, the latter as thick as the tibiae, middle and hind femora and tibiae of female ciliate both sides with nearly erect scales; wings grayish hyaline, tinged with pale yellowish at the bases, stigma dark brown, last section of fifth vein about one and one-half times as long as the preceding section. Length 4 to 5 mm. Four males and six females.

Habitat.—Sitka, June 16; Yakutat, June 21; Virgin Bay, June 26; Kadiak, Alaska, July 20. *Type.*—Cat. no. 5226, U. S. National Museum.

Near *Jlexuosa,* but in that species the mesonotum is nearly opaque, not black vittate; the legs and abdomen are dark brown, and the legs of the female are not ciliate with scales.

Rhamphomyia albopilosa sp. nov.

Black, the knobs of the halteres yellow, hairs white, many of those on the mesonotum, the ten marginal ones on the scutellum, those on the antennae, palpi, upper part of occiput, vertex, tibia, and tarsi, black; hairs on mesonotum and sides of abdomen abundant and

rather long; eyes of male contiguous, third joint of antennae two and onehalf times as long as broad, slightly over twice as long as the style; proboscis slightly longer than height of head; mesonotum slightly polished, the sides, front end and pleura opaque, gray pruinose; scutellum and abdomen polished, venter opaque, gray pruinose, hind margin of sixth ventral segment densely fringed with rather short yellowish bristles, the following ventral segment bearing a pair of bluntpointed, elongate, conical processes; hypopygium small, ascending, thinly pilose, claspers somewhat elongate oval, pointed at the apex, filament robust, usually free, the exposed portion somewhat shorter than the first joint of the hind tarsi, the latter thicker than that of any of the other tarsi, as thick as the tibiae, the first joint of the front and hind tarsi bearing many long hairs on the upper side; wings hyaline, veins and stigma dark brown, last section of fifth vein over twice as long as the preceding section, sixth vein prolonged to the wing margin. Length 5 mm. Two males, collected June 10.

Habitat.—Berg Bay, Alaska. *Type.*—Cat. no. 5227, U. S. National Museum.

Near *gilvipilosa,* but in that species the mesonotum is opaque, the abdomen nearly so, the scutellum bears only two bristles, and the venter of the abdomen is destitute of a fringe and pair of subconical processes.

Rhamphomyia adversa sp. nov.

Black, the halteres and bases of femora yellow, hairs and bristles black; third joint of antennae four times as long as broad, about five times as long as the style, proboscis slightly longer than height of head; thorax opaque, gray pruinose, mesonotum marked with three black vittae, scutellum bearing six bristles, abdomen slightly polished, almost bare, legs slender, nearly bare, first joint of hind tarsi much thicker than that of any of the other tarsi; wings very broad, black, the base about to apex of basal cells hyaline, venation normal, last section of fifth vein almost twice as long as the preceding section, sixth vein prolonged to the wing margin. Length 3 mm. Ten female specimens.

Habitat.—Sitka, June 16; Yakutat, June 21; Orca, Alaska, June 27. *Type.*—Cat. no. 5228, U. S. National Museum.

Closely related to *angustipennis,* but in that species the third joint of the antennae is only about twice as long as wide and twice as long as the style, and the median vitta on the mesonotum is light gray, instead of black.

Rhamphomyia cinefacta sp. nov.

Black, including the hairs; eyes of male contiguous, third joint of antennae about three times as long as wide, four times as long as the style, proboscis about twice as long as height of head; body opaque, gray pruinose, mesonotum not black vittate, its hairs and those of abdomen of female short and sparse, on abdomen of male abundant and rather long, scutellum bearing from four to six bristles, hypopygium rather small, ascending, claspers suboval, apex of dorsal piece bearing three or four very short spinous processes, filament rather robust toward the base, gradually tapering to the apex, the exposed portion slightly shorter than the first joint of the hind tarsi, the latter noticeably thicker than that of any of the other tarsi; hind tibiae of male bearing several rather long hairs on the outer and inner sides; wings of male hyaline, stigma and veins dark brown, in the female wholly pale brown, stigma slightly darker, in both sexes venation normal, last section of fifth vein almost twice as long as the preceding section, sixth vein obliterated before reaching the wing margin. Length 2.5 to 4 mm. Two males and one female, collected June 16.

Habitat.—Sitka, Alaska. *Type.*—Cat. no. 5229, U. S. National Museum.

Near *setosa,* but in that species the sixth vein is prolonged to the wing margin, and the dorsal piece of the male hypopygium is destitute of spinous processes at its apex.

Rhamphomyia setosa Coquillett.

Rhamphomyia setosa Coquillett, Proc. U. S. Nat. Museum, p. 426, 1896.

Berg Bay, June 10; Yakutat, June 21; Popof Island, July 8 and 10; Saldovia, July 21; Juneau, Alaska, July 26: Nine specimens of both sexes. This species was originally described from the White

Mountains, New Hampshire. In the original description, two errors occur, due to.imperfect or abnormal specimens which served for the type and co-types; the middle lamellae, or claspers, do not bear a process before their tips, the appearance in the type specimen being due to a matting of the bristly hairs at this point, and the enlarged base of the filament is present in most if not in all of the species, but in normal specimens is concealed from view.

Rhamphomyia anthracodes sp. nov.

Black, the hairs of the male abdomen, except dorsally, light yellow; eyes of the male separated almost as widely as the posterior ocelli, third joint of antennae slightly over twice as long as wide, three times as long as the style, proboscis slightly longer than height of head, body polished, mesonotum not distinctly vittate, its hairs sparse and rather short, scutellum bearing from four to six hairs, abdomen of male bearing many long hairs along the sides, hypopygium very large, ascending, claspers inverted subtriangular, the base truncate, the apex convex, the posterior margin rather densely fringed with long, yellowish, bristly hairs, emargination at apex of dorsal piece not reaching half way to its center, filament thread-like, the exposed portion about one and one-half times as long as the first joint of the hind tarsi, a rather strong curvature a short distance from the base; legs robust, hind tibiae of male fringed with long hairs on the outer and inner sides, first joint of hind tarsi subequal in thickness to that of the front ones, its upper edge fringed with rather long hairs, in the female the middle and hind femora and their tibiae are fringed on both sides with nearly erect scales; wings of male hyaline, of female pale brown, more yellowish brown at the base, in both the veins and stigma dark brown, venation normal, sixth vein obliterated before reaching the wing margin. Length 4 to 5 mm. Two males and one female. Habitat.—Metlakahtla, June 4; Sitka, Alaska, June 16. Type.—Cat. no. 5230, U. S. National Museum.

Rhamphomyia atrata sp. nov.

Black, including the hairs; eyes of male contiguous, third joint of antennae slightly over three times as long as broad, about three times as long as the style, proboscis twice as long as height of head, body opaque, mesonotum not vittate, its hairs quite abundant and long, scutellum bearing six bristles, hairs on sides of abdomen quite numerous and rather long, hypopygium small, obliquely ascending, claspers of nearly uniform width, the outer lower corner considerably prolonged, dorsal piece cleft from apex to beyond the center, filament rather robust, the exposed portion nearly straight, slightly less than half as long as the first joint of the hind tarsi, the latter about twice as thick as that of any of the other tarsi; hairs on outer side of hind tibias sparse and rather short, the inner side only pubescent; wings grayish hyaline, veins and stigma dark brown, last section of fifth vein over three times as long as the preceding section, sixth vein prolonged to the wing margin. Length 3mm. A male specimen, collected June 16. Habitat.—Sitka, Alaska.

Type.—Cat. no. 5231, U. S. National Museum. Rhamphomyia macrura sp. nov.

Black, the hairs also black, stems of halteres yellow, the knobs brown; eyes of male contiguous, third joint of antennae four times as long as wide, six times as long as the style, proboscis slightly longer than height of head; thorax opaque, gray pruinose, mesonotum marked with three slightly polished, black vittae, its hairs sparse and rather long, scutellum bearing six bristles, abdomen slightly polished, thinly gray pruinose, rather thickly covered with long hairs, hypopygium unusually long, ascending, claspers subtriangular, very sparsely covered with long hairs, at the apex bearing an elongate ovate process, like a second joint, more than one-third as long as the basal part and densely beset with long hairs on the lower side and apex, filament bristle-like, the exposed portion over five times as long as the first joint of the hind tarsi; hairs of hind tibiae sparse and rather short, first joint of front tarsi sublanceolate, thicker than the tibiae and nearly twice as thick

as that of the hind tarsi; wings grayish, pale smoky in the costal cell, stigma and veins dark brown, last section of fifth vein one and onehalf times as long as the preceding section, sixth vein prolonged to the wing margin. Length 4 to 5 mm. Ten males. Habitat.—Sitka, June 16; Yakutat, June 21; Virgin Bay, June 26; Orca, Alaska, June 27. Type.—Cat. no. 5232, U. S. National Museum.

Near clavigera, but in that species the first joint of the front tarsi is not thickened.

Ocydromia glabricula (Fallen).

Empis glabricula Fallen, Diptera Sueciae, Empidae, p. 33, 1816.

Sitka, Alaska: A single specimen, taken June 16. This European species was reported as occurring in this country twenty-two years ago. The U. S. National Museum contains a specimen collected in Colorado.

Platypalpus lateralis Loew.

Platypalpus lateralis Loew, Berliner Ent. Zeitsch., p. 89, 1864.

Muir Inlet, June 12; Sitka, June 16; Yakutat, June 21; Popof Proc. Wash. Acad. Scl., Norember, 1900.

Island, Alaska, July 8 to 12: Twenty-three specimens. The type locality of this species is the White Mountains, New Hampshire.

Platypalpus fiavirostris Loew.

Platypalpus flavirostris Loew, Berliner Ent. Zeitsch., p. 90, 1864.

Popof Island, Alaska: Five specimens, collected July 8 to 11. The type locality of this species is also the White Mountains, New Hampshire. Some of the specimens have the head yellow, as in P. tersus Coq., from which they may readily be distinguished by the broad front; in both sexes the front at its narrowest part is about one-third as wide as the distance from the lowest ocellus to the insertion of the antennae, greatly widening upwardly, whereas, in tersus the front only slightly widens upwardly, and at its narrowest point is only about oneeighth as wide as the distance from the lowest ocellus to the antennae.

Platypalpus diversipes sp. nov.

Black, the palpi and halteres whitish, legs yellow, bases of coxae, upper side of front femora, broad apices of other femora, of the tibiae and whole of tarsi, except base of the first joint, black; head polished, the face opaque, whitish pruinose, third joint of antennae only slightly longer than broad, body polished, pleura opaque, thinly gray pruinose; front femora considerably thickened, about two thirds as thick as the middle ones; wings hyaline, veins yellowish brown, first and second basal cells subequal in length. Length 1.5 mm. Three males and twelve females, collected July 8 to 13.

Habitat.—Popof Island, Alaska. *Type.* —Cat. no. 5233, U. S. National Museum.

Platypalpus gilvipes sp. nov.

Black, the first two joints of antennae, palpi, halteres and legs, including the coxae, yellow, last joint of tarsi brown; third joint of antennae about twice as long as wide, head polished, the face opaque, white pruinose, body polished, the front end of pleura to posterior side of front coxae, also the lateral margins of metanotum, encroaching slightly on the pleura, opaque, gray pruinose; front femora noticeably thickened, about two-thirds as thick as the middle ones; wings hyaline, veins brown, first and second basal cells subequal in length. Length 2 to nearly 3 mm. Four males and five females, collected July 8 to 12.

Habitat.—Popof Island, Alaska. *Type.* —Cat. no. 5234, U. S. National Museum.

Closely related to *lateralis,* but in that species the entire pleura, except a spot above the middle coxae, is opaque, gray pruinose, and the entire antennae are brown or black.

Phoneutisca bimaculata Loew.

Phoneutisca bimaculata Loew, Berliner Ent. Zeitsch., p. 19, 1863.
Muir Inlet, Alaska: Seven specimens, taken June 12. Originally described from Alaska.

Sciodromia bicolor (Loew).

Synamphotera bicolor Loew, Berliner Ent. Zeitsch., p. 18, 1863.
Popof Island, Alaska: Two specimens, collected July 8 and 12. Originally described from Alaska.

Mantipeza valida (Loew).

Hemerodromia valida Loew, Berliner Ent. Zeitsch., p. 208, 1862.
Popof Island, Alaska: A single specimen, captured July 9. This species was originally described from the region about Hudson Bay, British America.

Family DOLICHOPODHXffi. Dolichopus discifer Stannius.

Dolichopus discifer Stannius, Isis, p. 57, 1831.—Schiner, Fauna Austriaca, Dipt., 1, p. 216, 1862.—Loew, Monographs Dipt. N. Am., 11, p. 71, 1864.
Dolichopus tanypus Loew, Neue Beitr. Kennt. Dipt., VI11, p. 24, 1861.
Kukak Bay, July 4; Popof Island, July 8 to 11; Kadiak, July 21; Juneau, Alaska, July 26: Twenty-seven specimens. This European species was reported by Dr. Loew to occur in New Hampshire, the southern part of British America and in Alaska about twenty-six years ago, and Osten Sacken has also recorded it from New York.

Dolichopus plumipes (Scopoli).

Musca plumipes Scopoli, Entomol. Cam, p. 334, 1763. *Dolichopus plumipes* Schiner, Fauna Austriaca, Dipt., 1, p. 217, 1862.—
Loew, Monog. N. Am. Dipt., 11, p. 60, 1864. *Dolichopus pennitarsis* Fallen, Diptera Sueciae, Dolichopidae, p. 11, 1823.

Sitka, June 16; Yakutat, June 21; Virgin Bay, June 23; Kukak Bay, July 4; Popof Island, July 8 to 10; Kadiak, July 20; Saldovia, Alaska, July 21: Forty specimens. Also a European species, reported by Dr. Loew as occurring in Alaska about twenty-six years ago. It has also been recorded from Canada, South Dakota, and Colorado.

Dolichopus xanthocnemus Loew.

Dolichopus xanthocnemus Loew, Monog. N. Am. Dipt., 11, p. 31, 1864.
Kukak Bay, July 4; Popof Island, July 8 to 12; Kadiak, July 20; Saldovia, Alaska, July 21: Forty-four specimens. Originally described from Alaska. Dolichopus stenhammari Zetterstedt.

Dolichopus stenkammari Zetterstedt, Diptera Scand., 11, p. 521, 1843.
Muir Inlet, June 12; Sitka, June 16; Virgin Bay, June 26; Kukak Bay, Alaska, July 4: Eleven specimens. This Euro-

pean species has been reported from Labrador by Osten Sacken.

Dolichopus festinans Zetterstedt.

Dolichopus festinans Zetterstedt, Diptera Scand., 11, p. 507, 1843.
Kukak Bay, July 3; Popof Island, Alaska, July 8 and 9: Four specimens of both sexes. This European species has not heretofore been reported as occurring on this Continent.

Dolichopus barycnemus sp. nov.

Front brassy green, face yellowish gray pruinose, antenna black, the lower side of the first joint reddish yellow, the third joint ovate, palpi yellow, bristles of sides of occiput yellowish white; body bluish green, tinged in places with brassy, lamellae of hypopygium white, bordered with black, remainder of hypopygium black; front coxae yellow, a black, gray pruinose spot at base of outer side, middle and hind coxa black, gray pruinose, their apices yellow; femora yellow, apices of hind ones black, and with a bristle on the outer side before the tip, front and middle femora bare on the under side, the hind ones ciliate with rather long, black hairs on the median third; front and middle tibiae yellow, the hind ones, except their extreme bases, black and greatly swollen, more than twice as thick as either of the other tibiae, all tibiae bearing many bristles; front tarsi yellow on the first three joints, the remainder black and somewhat compressed, fourth joint slightly dilated, the fifth still more so but less than twice as broad as the third; middle tarsi black, the first joint, except the apex, yellow, about as long as the remaining joints taken together; hind tarsi black, much more robust than the others; halteres yellow, bristles of calypteres black; wings grayish hyaline, smoky brown in front of the third vein, an elongated thickening of the costa at apex of first vein, fourth vein not broken; length 6 mm. A male specimen, collected July 11.

Habitat.—Popof Island, Alaska. *Type.* —Cat. no. 5235, U. S. National Museum.

Closely related to the European *D. atritibialis* Zetterstedt, but the latter is credited with having the antennae yellow, the apex and upper side of the third joint black, the face silvery white pruinose and the hind femora bare on the under side. Dolichopus varipes sp. nov.

Differs from the above description of *barycnemus* only as follows: Lower half of first two joints of antennae yellow, fore coxae wholly yellow, hind femora wholly black, only pubescent on the under side, middle femora each with a black spot on the median third of the under side, hind tibiae only slightly swollen, yellow, the apical sixth (less on the outer side) brownish black, last two joints of front tarsi not compressed nor dilated, first joint of middle tarsi shorter than the three succeeding joints taken together, the first three joints slender, yellow, the two others black, compressed and fringed with bristles on the upper side, the fourth joint twice as wide as the third, slightly wider and one-third longer than the fifth; wings wholly hyaline, costa not thickened at apex of first vein; female as in the male except that the middle tarsi are like the front ones. Length about 5 mm. A specimen of each sex, collected July 8 and 10.

Habitat.—Popof Island, Alaska. *Type.* —Cat. no. 5236, U. S. National Museum.
Differs in the coloring of the femora from any other species known to me.

Dolichopus longimanus Loew.
Dolichopus longimanus Loew, Neue Beitr. Kennt. Dipt., vI11, p. 14, 1861. Monog. Dipt. N. Am., 11, p. 38, 1864.
Metlakahtla, in June; Kukak Bay, July 4; Kadiak, Alaska, July 20: Twenty-seven specimens. Originally described from English
River, British America; it has also been reported from New York,
New Hampshire, and South Dakota.

Dolichopus plumitarsis Fallen.
Dolichopus plumitarsis Fallen, Diptera Sueciae, Dolich., p. 10, 1823.— Schiner, Fauna Austriaca, Dipt., 1, p.216, 1862.—Zetterstedt, Dipt. Scand., 11, p. 556, 1843.
Kukak Bay, July 4; Popof Island, Alaska, July 10: Three male specimens. A European species, not heretofore reported from this Continent.

Dolichopus lobatus Loew.
Dolichopus lobatus Loew, Neue Beitr. Kennt. Dipt., v11i, p. 24, 1861. Monog. Dipt. N. Am., 11, p. 72, 1864.
Kukak Bay, Alaska: A specimen of each sex, taken July 4. Originally described from English River, British America, and also reported from South Dakota, Illinois, and Michigan.

Porphyrops consobrinus Zetterstedt.
Porphyrops consobrinus Zetterstedt, Dipt. Scand., 11, p. 471, 1843; vm, p. 3061, 1849.
Yakutat, June 21; Kukak Bay, Alaska, July 4: A specimen of each sex. This is a European species, not heretofore reported as occurring on this Continent.

Sympycnus cuprinus Wheeler.
Sympycnus cuprinus Wheeler, Proc. Cal. Acad. Sciences, p. 50, 1899.
Popof Island, July 10 to 12; Juneau, Alaska, July 25 and 26: Seven specimens. Originally described from the vicinity of Monterey, Calif.

Hydrophorus glaber (Walker).
Medeterus glaber Walker, List Dipt. Ins. Brit. Museum, m, p. 655, 1849.
Metlakahtla, Alaska: A single specimen, collected June 4. Originally described from Albany River, British America.

Family SYRPHHXE. Pipiza pisticoides Williston.
Pipiza pisticoides Williston, Synopsis N. Am. Syrphidse, p. 29, 1886.
Fox Point, Alaska: Three specimens, collected July 28. Originally described from New Hampshire; the U. S. National Museum also contains specimens from Maine, New York, and Colorado.

Chilosia occidentalis Williston.
Chilosia occidentalis Williston, Proc. Am. Phil. Soc., p. 305, 1882. Synopsis N. Am. Syrphidae, p. 41, 1886.
Virgin Bay, June 25; Popof Island, Alaska, July 10 and 12: Three specimens. Originally described from California; there is also a specimen in the U. S. National Museum from Colorado.

Chilosia borealis sp. nov.
Male: Head black; frontal triangle sulcate in middle, its hairs black, those of the vertex mixed yellow and black; face polished, the upper margin and narrow border to the eyes gray pruinose,

hairs along the eyes short, sparse, whitish, median portion of face bare, central tubercle prominent, a deep, concave space below it, the oral margin protruding, face only slightly produced downward; first two joints of antennae black, the third dark brown, orbicular, as wide as long, the arista black, almost bare; eyes densely covered with rather long yellowish or black hairs; body greenish black, polished, the hairs mixed yellow and black, on front part of mesonotum and sides of abdomen chiefly yellow, scutellum bearing several marginal black, bristly hairs, second and third segments of abdomen, except the sides and front angles, of a purer black color, venter polished, its hairs yellow; legs black, extreme apices of the femora, broad bases and narrower apices of the tibiae yellow; halteres yellow, center of the knobs brown; wings grayish hyaline, sometimes tinged with yellow on the costo-basal half, the veins brown, stigma pale yellowish.

Female: Differs from the male as follows: Hairs of front and of body almost wholly yellow, front not sulcate, abdomen destitute of purer black portions, halteres wholly light yellow. Length 5 to 7 mm. Four males and seventeen females.
Habitat.—Yakutat, June 21; Virgin Bay, June 25; Kukak Bay, July 1 and 4; Kadiak, July 20; Saldovia, Alaska, July 21. *Type.*—Cat. no. 5237, U. S. National Museum.
Closely related to *occidentalism* but in that species the sides of the median portion of the face are hairy, and the size is much larger.

Chilosia alaskensis Hunter.
Chilosia alaskensis Hunter, Canadian Entom., p. 124, 1897.
Yakutat, Alaska: A single specimen, collected June 21. Originally described from Alaska.

Chilosia lasiophthalma Williston.
Chilosia lasiophthalma Williston, Proc. Am. Phil. Soc., p. 306, 1882. Synopsis N. Am. Syrphidae, p. 40, 1886.
Yakutat, June 21; Kukak Bay, Alaska, July 1: Five specimens. Originally described from Colorado.

Chilosia tristis Loew.

Chilosia tristis Loew, Berliner Entom. Zeitsch., p. 312, 1863.

Saldovia, Alaska, July 21: Three specimens. Originally described from the Red River, British America.

Chilosia plutonia Hunter.

Chilosiaplutonia Hunter, Canadian Ent. , p. 125, 1897.

Chilosia gracilis Hunter, loc. cit., p. 126.

Sitka, June 16; Yakutat, June 21; Virgin Bay, June 26; Kukak Bay, July 1 and 4; Popof Island, July 8 to 15; Kadiak, July 20; Saldovia, July 21; Fox Point, Alaska, July 28: Seventy-two specimens, of both sexes. Originally described from Alaska, the two sexes having been described as separate species.

Chilosia pulchripes Loew.

Chilosia pulchripes Loew, Verhandlungen Zool.-Bot. Vereins. p. 19, 1857.—Schiner, Fauna Austr., Dipt., 1, p. 281, 1862.—Becker, Revision Gatt. Chilosia, p. 372, 1894.

Kukak Bay, July 1 and 4; Saldovia, Alaska, July 21: Nine specimens. A European species, not heretofore reported as occurring on this Continent.

Melanostoma mellinum (Linnd).

Mutca mellinum Linne, Fauna Suec., p. 1820, 1761. *Melanostoma mellinum* Schiner, Fauna Austriaca, Dipt., I, p. 291, 1862.— Williston, Synopsis N. Am. yrphidae, p. 49, 1886.

Metlakahtla, June 4; Berg Bay, June 10; Sitka, June 16; Yakutat, June 21; Virgin Bay, June 26; Kukak Bay, July 1; Popof Island, July 8 to 15; Kadiak, July 20; Saldovia, July 21; Juneau, July 25; Fox Point, Alaska, July 28: One hundred and fifty-one specimens. This is also a European species reported as occurring on this Continent from Canada and Alaska, on the north, to Argentina, South America, on the south.

Melanostoma trichopus Thomson.

Syrphus trichopus Thomson, Kongliga Sven. Freg. Eng. Resa, p. 502, 1868.

Metlakahtla, June 4; Kukak Bay, July 1; Popof Island, Alaska, July 8 and 9. Four specimens. Originally described from California.

Platychirus peltatus (Meigen).

Syrphuspeltatus Meigen, Syst. Besch. Eur. Zweif. Ins., i11, p. 334, 1822.

Ptatychiruspeltatus Schiner, Fauna Aust, Diptera, 1, p. 295,1862.—WillisTon. Synopsis N. Am. Syrphidae, p. 58, 1886.

Lowe Inlet, British Columbia, June 3; Sitka, June 16; Kukak Bay, July 1; Popof Island, July 8 to 14; Fox Point, Alaska, July 28: Nineteen specimens. A European species heretofore reported as occurring in this country from New Hampshire and Pennsylvania to Alaska and Colorado. Platychirus tenebrosus sp. nov.

Male: Head black, its hairs black, those on lower part of occiput whitish, sides of frontal triangle bronze green, head at anterior oral margin noticeably shorter than at base of antennae, face polished, the tubercle very small; antennae black, the third joint dark brown, slightly longer than wide, mouth parts polished black; thorax and scutellum black, polished, the hairs mixed yellow and black, a whitish pruinose spot on lower part of the sternopleura and metapleura; abdomen black, somewhat velvety, opaque, the first segment, sides of abdomen except hind angles of the third and fourth segment, also the fifth segment and genitalia, polished and having a brassy tinge, a pair of yellow spots on the second, third, and fourth segments, not touching the front nor lateral margin of the segments, those on the second the smallest, nearly circular, on the third segment the largest, elliptical, extending lengthwise with the segment, those on the fourth rhomboidal; front legs yellow, the coxae, posterior side of the femora except at the apex, and a streak on outer side of the tibia:, black, apices of tibiae and the first tarsal joint except its apex, whitish, tibiae greatly dilated at the apex, on the inner side gradually dilated for three-fourths of its length, then slightly narrowed to the apex, on the outer side rather abruptly dilated on the last third of its length, slightly narrowing to the apex, the outer angle prolonged considerably beyond the inner; tarsi dilated, tapering gradually to the fourth joint, the latter slightly narrower than the fifth, the first joint about two-thirds as wide as broadest part of the tibiae, about one and one-half times as

long as broad, femora on the posterior and under sides bearing many rather long black bristly hairs, the tibiae and tarsi destitute of hairs; middle and hind legs black, the knees and apices of the tibiae yellowish, femora bearing many rather long hairs, the tibiae and tarsi destitute of them; wings grayish-hyaline, brownish at base and tinged with smoky along the anterior veins, stigma yellow, halteres also yellow.

Female: Differs from the male as follows: Hairs of head largely yellow, front tinged with bronze, face, except the tubercle, grayish pruinose, extending on sides of front to its middle where it is conically expanded toward the center of the front, thorax and scutellum tinged with bronze, their hairs yellow; abdomen bronze black, polished, the yellow spots nearly circular; front tibiae gradually and moderately dilated, their tarsi noticeably widened, middle femora, their tibiae, and first two joints of their tarsi, yellow, both ends of the hind femora and tibiae also yellow, wings not brown at base nor tinged with smoky. Length 7 mm. One male and two females.

Habitat.—Kukak Bay, July 1; Popof Island, July 8; Kadiak, Alaska, July 28. *Type.*—Cat. no. 5238, U. S. National Museum.

Readily recognized by the shortness of the lower part of the head, the remoteness of the abdominal yellow spots from the margins of the segments, the absence of hooked bristles on the front femora of the male, his simple middle tibiae and the absence of bristly hairs on all the tibiae.

Platychirus aeratus sp. nov.

Male: Differs from the above description of *tenebrosus* only as follows: Frontal triangle and face, except the tubercle, thinly grayish pruinose, thorax and scutellum bronze black, the hairs yellow; abdomen marked with a pair of gray pruinose, bronze colored, subelliptical spots at the anterior outer angles of the third and fourth segments; front femora, except the apices, black, their tibiae gradually and moderately dilated toward the apices, their tarsi only moderately dilated and of nearly an equal width, the first joint almost as wide as broadest part of the tibiae, about twice as long as wide; middle tarsi brownish yellow, the bases broadly yellow.

Female: Resembles the male with these exceptions: Lower half of front thinly gray pruinose, most dense along the eyes, abdomen polished and destitute of spots; front femora sometimes yellow except on the outer side, their tibiae only slightly dilated, middle femora, tibiae, and tarsi sometimes yellow except on posterior sides of femora, wings pure hyaline. Length 5 to 7 mm.

Two males and two females, collected June 12.
Habitat.—Muir Inlet, Alaska. *Type.*—Cat. no. 5239, U. S. National Museum. A very slender species, closely related to *albimanus,* but in the latter the head is much longer at the anterior oral margin than at base of antennae, the front femora of the male bear several hooked bristles on the posterior side before the middle, his front and middle tibiae have several rather long bristly hairs on the outer side, and the abdomen of the female is spotted nearly the same as in the male.

Platychirus albimanus (Fabricius).
Syrphusalbimanus Fabricius, Species Insectorum, 11, p. 434, 1781.
Platychirus albimanus Schiner, Fauna Austr., Diptera, I, p. 294, 1862.
Sitka, June 16; Popof Island, Alaska, July 14 and 16: Three males and one female. A European species, not heretofore reported from this Continent.

Leucozona leucorum (Linne).
Musca leucorum Linne, Fauna Suecica, p. 1803, 1761.
Leucozona leucorum Schiner, Fauna Austriaca, Diptera, I, p. 299, 1862.—Williston, Synopsis N Am. Syrphidae, p. 62, 1886.
Popof Island, July 13; Saldovia, July 21; Juneau, Alaska, July 25: Three specimens. Also a European species, hitherto reported as occurring in Canada, Colorado, and Washington.

Syrphus axcuatus (Fallen).
Scava arcuata Fallen, Diptera Sueciae, Syrphidae, p. 42, 1816. *Syrphus arcuatus* Schiner, Fauna Austriaca, Dipt., I, p. 305, 1862.—WillisTon Synopsis N.

Am. Syrphidae, p. 68, 1886.
Popof Island, July 10; Saldovia, July 21; Juneau, Alaska, July 25: Three specimens. A European species, heretofore reported as occurring over the northern portion of this Continent, extending southward as far as Virginia and New Mexico.

Syrphus amalopis Osten Sacken.
Syrphus amalopis Osten Sacken, Proc. Boston Soc. Nat. Hist., p. 148, 1875.—Williston, Synopsis N. Am. Syrphidae, p. 69, 1886.
Sitka, June 16; Yakutat, June 21; Virgin Bay, June 26; Kukak Bay, July 1; Saldovia, July 21; Juneau, July 25; Fox Point, Alaska, July 28: Thirty-six specimens. Originally described from New Hampshire.

Syrphus contumax. Osten Sacken.
Syrphus contumax Osten Sacken, Proc. Boston Soc. Nat. Hist., p. 148, 1875.—Williston, Synopsis N. Am. Syrphidae, p. 71, 1886. *Syrphus bryantii* Johnson, Entom News, p. 17, 1898.
Berg Bay, June 10; Muir Inlet, June 12; Kukak Bay, July 1; Popof Island, Alaska, July 8 to 11: Thirty-five specimens. This species was also originally described from New Hampshire; the type of *bryantii* was collected in Alaska, and Mr. Johnson has confirmed the above synonymy in a recent letter.

Syrphus mentalis Williston.
Syrphus mentalis Williston, Synopsis N. Am. Syrphidae, p. 72, 1886.
Virgin Bay, June 26; Kukak Bay, Alaska, July 1: Two specimens. Originally described from Washington. Its occurrence in Alaska has already been recorded by Mr. W. D. Hunter.

Syrphus velutinus Williston.
Syrphus velutinus Williston, Proc. Am. Phil. Soc., p. 314, 1882. Synopsis N. Am. Syrphidae, p. 73, 1886.
Fox Point, Alaska: A single specimen, captured July 28. The type locality is Oregon.

Syrphus diversipes Macquart.
Syrphus diversipes Macquart, Dipteres Exotiques, 4 Sup., p. 155, 1849.— Williston, Synopsis N. Am. Syrphidae, p. 76, 1886.
Sitka, June 16; Yakutat, June 21; Virgin Bay, June 16; Saldovia, Alaska, July 21:

Twenty-seven specimens. Originally described from Newfoundland; it has also been reported from New Hampshire, New York, the shores of Lake Superior, and Washington. A specimen in the U. S. National Museum was collected in Colorado.

Syrphus gracilis sp. nov.
Front polished, black, with a brassy tinge, not pruinose, its hairs black; face polished yellow, a broad median vitta, the oral margin, and cheeks black, the hairs black, those on upper part of occiput yellowish, on the lower part white; eyes bare, antennae black, mouth parts dark brown, facial tubercle very prominent; thorax polished, metallic bluish bronze, its hairs light colored; scutellum polished, yellow, with a metallic bluish reflection, its hairs black; abdomen polished, black, a pair of small, orbicular, yellow spots on the second segment, situated in front of the middle and close to the lateral margins, posterior margin of the fourth segment and front angles of the fifth, yellow; legs black, apices of front femora and bases of front tibiae brownish yellow; halteres yellow, the stems brown; wings hyaline, stigma brown. Length 7 mm. A female specimen collected July 25.
Habitat.—Juneau, Alaska. *Type.*—Cat. no. 5240, U. S. National Museum.
An unusually slender species, easily recognized by the polished, not pruinose front, and absence of yellow markings on the third abdominal segment.

Syrphus ribesii (Linne).
Afusca ribesii Linne, Fauna Suec., p. 1816, 1761. *Syrphus ribesii* Schiner, Fauna Austriaca, Dipt.. I, p. 310, 1862. —WillisTon, Synopsis N. Am. Syrphidae, p. 77, 1886.
Metlakahtla, June 4; Popof Island, July 8 to 15; Juneau, July 25; Fox Point, Alaska, July 28: Nine specimens. A European species, reported as occurring over the greater portion of this Continent, from Washington on the north to Argentina, South America, on the south.

Syrphus torvus Osten Sacken.
Syrphus torvus Osten Sacken, Proc. Boston Soc. Nat. Hist., p. 139, 1875.—Williston, Synopsis N. Am, Syrphidae, p. 79, 1886.

Juneau, June 25; Kukak Bay, July 21; Popof Island, Alaska, July 8 to 10: Seven specimens. Also a European species. It has been recorded as occurring in Siberia, while on this Continent its reported range is from Greenland to Rhode Island, and in the West from Washington to Colorado. The U. S. National Museum contains several specimens which are labeled as having been collected in North Carolina and'Georgia.

Syrphus geniculatus Macquart.

Syrphus geniculatus Macquart, Dipteres Exot., 11, Part 2, p. 101, 1841.— Williston, Synopsis N. Am. Syrphidae, p. 84, 1886.

Kukak Bay, July 1; Popof Island, Alaska, July 8 to 15: Four specimens. Originally described from Newfoundland; it has also been reported from New Hampshire and Alaska.

Syrphus glacialis (Johnson).

Melanostoma glacialis Johnson, Entom. News, p. 18, 1898.

Berg Bay, June 10; Yakutat, June 21; Kukak Bay, July 4; Popof Island, July 8 to 13; Kadiak, Alaska, July 20: Nine specimens. The type locality of this species is Alaska.

Syrphus macularis (Zetterstedt).

Scava macularis Zetterstedt, Diptera Scand., 11, p. 730, 1843.

Yakutat, Alaska: Eight specimens, of both sexes, collected June 21. A European species, not heretofore recorded as occurring on this Continent.

Didea laza Osten Sacken.

Didea laxa Osten Sacken, Bulletin Buffalo Soc. Nat. Hist., p. 56, 1875.

Saldovia, Alaska: A single specimen, collected July 21. The specimens on which the original description was founded were collected in Maine, New Hampshire, and on the shores of Lake Superior. In the West, this species has been recorded as occurring from Washington to Mexico.

Sphaerophoria sulphuripes (Thomson).

Syrphus sulphuripes Thomson, Kongliga Sven. Freg. Eug. Resa, p. 501, 1868. *Sphcerophoria sulphuripes* Williston, Synopsis N. Am. Syrphidae, p. 106, 1886.

Fox Point, Alaska: A single specimen, taken July 28. Originally described from California.

Neoascia globosa (Walker).

Ascia globosa Walker, List Dipt. Ins. British Museum, I11, p. 546, 1849. *Neoascia globosa* Williston, Synopsis N. Am. Syrphidae, p. i11, 1886.

Metlakahtla, June 4; Virgin Bay, June 26; Popof Island, Alaska, July 8 to 18: Fourteen specimens. This species was originally described from New York, and has been reported from Connecticut and Oregon. The U. S. National Museum also contains a specimen collected in Colorado.

Sphegina infuscata Loew.

Sphegina infuscata Loew, Berliner Ent. Zeitsch., p. 13, 1863.—Willistom, Synopsis N. Am. Syrphidae, p. 114, 1886.

Lowe Inlet, British Columbia, June 3; Farragut Bay, June 5; Sitka, June 16; Yakutat, June 21; Virgin Bay, Alaska, June 26: Fortyeight specimens. The abdomen of the male is sometimes of the same color as that of the female. This species was originally described from Sitka, and has also been reported from Oregon. The U. S. National Museum contains specimens collected in Colorado and New Hampshire.

Baccha obscuricornis Loew.

B ace ha obscuricornis Loew, Berliner Ent. Zeitsch., p. 15, 1863.—Williston Synopsis N. Am. Syrphidae, p. 123, 1886.

Lowe Inlet, British Columbia, June 3; Sitka, Alaska, June 16:

Three specimens. Originally described from Sitka; it has also been reported from Oregon and New Mexico.

Myiolepta bella Williston.

MyioUpta bella Williston, Proc. Am. Phil. Soc., p. 308, 1882. Synopsis N. Am. Syrphidae, p. 128, 1886.

Virgin Bay, Alaska: A male specimen, collected June 26. Originally reported from Washington and Oregon.

Brachyopa notata Osten Sacken.

Brachyopa notata Osten Sacken, Bulletin Buffalo Soc. Nat. Hist., p. 68, 1875.—Williston, Synopsis N. Am. Syrphidae, p. 132, 1886.

Sitka, June 16; Yakutat, June 21; Virgin

Bay, Alaska, June 26: Ten specimens. Originally described from New Hampshire, and also recorded from Washington and Oregon. Arctophila fiagrans Osten Sacken.

ArctopHla fiagrans Osten Sacken, Bulletin Buffalo Soc. Nat. Sci., p. 69, 1875. —Williston, Synopsis N. Am. Syrphidae, p. 158, 1886.

Popof Island, Alaska: A single specimen, collected July 10. This species was originally described from Colorado, and has been reported from New Mexico. Volucella facialis Williston.

Volucella facialis Williston, Proc. Am. Phil. So, p. 316, 1882. Synopsis N. Am. Syrphidae, p. 137, 1886.

Kukak Bay, July 1; Popof Island, July 13; Kadiak, July 20;

Saldovia, Alaska, July 21: Thirjteen specimens. The type locality of this species is in California, and the species has also been recorded from Colorado.

Sericomyia chalcopyga Loew.

Sericomyia chalcopyga Loew, Berliner Ent. Zeitsch., p. 12, 1863.—WillisTon, Synopsis N. Am. Syrphidae, p. 156, 1886.

Sitka, June 16; Fox Point, Alaska, July 28: Eight specimens. Originally described from Sitka; it has been reported from Washington and Oregon. The U. S. National Museum also contains a specimen collected by Mrs. A. T. Slosson, at Franconia, New Hampshire.

Eristalis meigenii Wiedemann.

Eristalis meigenii Wiedemann, Ausser. Zweif. Insekten, 11, p. 177, 1830. *Eristalis brousii* Williston, Proc. Am. Phil. Soc., p. 323, 1882. Synopsis N. Am. Syrphidae, p. 165, 1886.

Juneau, Alaska: Two specimens, collected July 25. This species was originally described from Uruguay, South America; it has also been reported as occurring from Alaska and Canada to Colorado and Pennsylvania. The synonymy is on the authority of Dr. Williston.

Eristalis occidentalis Williston.

Eristalis occidentals Williston, Proc. Am. Phil. Soc., p. 322, 1882. Synopsis N. Am. Syrphidae, p. 167, 1886.

Metlakahtla, June 4; Sitka, June 16; Virgin Bay, June 26; Kadiak, July 20;

Juneau, July 25; Fox Point, Alaska, July 28: Thirty-one specimens. This species was originally described from Washington, and has already been reported as occurring in Alaska.

Eristalis flavipes Walker.

Eristalis flavipes Walker, List Dipt. Ins. Brit. Museum, 111, p. 633, 1849.—Williston, Synopsis N. Am. Syrphidae, p. 168, 1886.

Fox Point, Alaska: A single specimen, captured July 28. Originally described from Albany River, British America; it has also been reported as occurring from Washington and Canada to Colorado and Rhode Island.

Eristalis compactus Walker.

Eristalis compactus WALKER, List Dipt. Ins. Brit. Museum i11, p 619, 1849.—Williston, Synopsis N. Am. Syrphidae, p 169, 1886.

Kadiak, Alaska: Two specimens, taken July 19 and 20. This species was originally described from Albany River, British America; it has also been recorded from Canada, New Hampshire, and Connecticut.

Eristalis obscurus Loew.

Eristaiis obscurus Loew, Berliner Ent. Zeitsch., p. 171, 1865.—Williston, Synopsis N. Am. Syrphidse, p. 175, 1886.

Fox Point, Alaska: Three specimens, captured July 28. Originally described from Red River, British America.

Helophilus lunulatus Meigen.

Helophilus lunulatus Meigen, System. Besch. Eur. Zweif. Insekten, Hi, p. 370, 1822.—Schiner, Fauna Austr., Dipt., I, p. 340, 1862.

Kadiak, Alaska: A single specimen, collected July 20. This is a European species, not heretofore reported as occurring on this Continent. Specimens are contained in the U. S. National Museum collection taken at Toronto and Ottawa, Canada, by Messrs. W. Brodie and W. H. Harrington. Four of these were received from Mr. Brodie under the name of *Helophilus canadensis* Brodie; this name appears in the published Check-list of the Insects of Canada, but no description accompanies the name, nor has any ever been published so far as I am aware.

Helophilus dychei Williston.

Helophilus dychei Williston, Canadian Ent., p. 136, 1897.'

Berg Bay, June 10; Kadiak, July 20; Juneau, July 25; Fox Point, Alaska, July 28: Ten specimens. Originally described from Alaska.

Criorhina annillata Osten Sacken.

Criorhina armillata Osten Sacken, Bulletin Buffalo Soc. Nat. Sci., p. 68, 1875.—Williston, Synopsis N. Am. Syrphidae, p. 213, 1886.

Fox Point, Alaska: A single specimen, collected July 28. The type locality of this species is Quebec, Canada. The U. S. National

Museum contains specimens from New Hampshire and Montana.

Criorhina scitula Williston.

Criorhina scitula Williston, Proc. Am. Phil. Soc., p. 331, 1882. Synopsis N. Am. Syrphidae, p. 215, 1886.

Fox Point, Alaska: A single specimen, captured July 28. Originally described from Washington. The U. S. National Museum also contains a specimen from Mt. Hood, Oregon.

Criorhina tricolor sp. nov.

Eyes of male separated as widely as the posterior ocelli, upper half of front brownish black, the lower half brownish yellow, on the sides broadly yellow pruinose, face yellow, opaque, yellow pruinose, deeply concave below the antennae, the lower portion strongly convex, cheeks polished, brownish black, antennae brownish yellow, upper side of third joint brownish black, first joint cylindrical, slightly longer than the second, the third transversely oval, nearly twice as wide as long, arista black, proboscis dark brown, rather short and robust; thorax and scutellum polished, bronze black, the hairs long and abundant, whitish, a transverse band of black ones behind middle of mesonotum; abdomen polished, the first two segments light yellow, covered with long, abundant whitish hairs, remainder of abdomen black, its hairs golden yellow; legs black, tibiaeyellowish, with a brown band before the middle and another near the tip, first three tarsal joints brownish yellow; wings hyaline, stigma grayish brown. Length 12 mm. A male speci-

men, collected June 16. *Habitat.*—Sitka, Alaska.

Type.—Cat. no. 5241, U. S. National Museum. Closely related to *coquilletti,* but in that species the first two segments of the abdomen are black, and covered with black hairs, etc.

Xylota barbata Loew.

Xylota barbata Loew, Berliner Ent. Zeitsch., p. 70, 1864.—Williston, Synopsis N. Am. Syrphidae, p. 233, 1886.

Juneau, Alaska: A single specimen, collected July 25. Originally described from Alaska, it has also been reported from Washington, Oregon, and California.

Family PHORID.E.

Trineura aterrima (Fabricius).

Musca aterrima Fabricius, Entom. System., iv, p. 334, 1794.

Trineura aterrima Schiner, Fauna Austriaca, Dipt., 11, p. 347, 1864.

Berg Bay, June 10; Muir Inlet, June 12; Sitka, June 16; Yakutat, June 21; Popof Island, July 8 to 12; Kadiak, July 20; Saldovia, Alaska, July 21: Twenty-seven specimens. A European species, first reported as occurring in this country about forty years ago. The U. S. National Museum contains specimens from the White Mountains, New Hampshire, and Summit County, Colorado.

Phora rufipes (Meigen).

Trineura rufipes Meigen, Klass. Besch. Eur. Zweif. Insekten, I, p. 313, 1804.

Phora rufipes Schiner, Fauna Austriaca, Dipt., 11, p. 340, 1864.

Muir Inlet, June 12; Sitka, Alaska, June 16: Two specimens. Also a European species, first recorded from this country at the same time as the preceding species.

Phora fungicola Coquillett.

Phora fungicola Coquillett, Canadian Ent, p. 106, 1895.

Proc. Wash. Acad. Sci. November, 1900.

Popof Island, Alaska: Three specimens, collected July 10, II, and 14. Originally described from New Mexico, it has also been recorded as occurring in New Jersey.

Family (ESTRID. (Edemagena tarandi (Linne).

Estrus tarandi Linn£, Fauna Suecica, p. 1731, 1761.—Zetterstedt, Dipt. Scand., i11, p. 973, 1844.

Popof Island, Alaska: A single specimen, captured July 12. This is a European species, first recorded from North America about fiftyeight years ago. The U. S. National Museum contains a specimen-collected at Point Barrow, Alaska, August 15, 1872, by Mr. John Murdock.

Family TACHINID.E. Thryptocera flavipes Coquillett.

Thryptocera flavipes Coquillett, Revision Tachinidae, p. 58, 1897.

Yakutat, June 21; Virgin Bay, June 26; Orca, Alaska, June 27: Thirty-five specimens. Originally described from the mountains of New Hampshire.

Didyma pullula van der Wulp.

Didyma pullula Van Der Wulp, Biologia Cent.-Amer., Diptera, 11, p. 162, 1S90.

Farragut Bay, Alaska: A single specimen, collected June I. The type locality of this species is in the high mountains of Guerrero, Mexico.

Linnaemyia picta (Meigen).

Tachina picta Meigen, Syst. Besch. Eur. Zweif. Insekten, iv, p. 261, 1824. *Micropalpus picta* Schiner, Fauna Aust., Diptera, I, p. 429, 1862. *Linncrmyia picta* Coquillett, Revision Tachinidae, p. 87, 1897.

Fox Point, Alaska: A single specimen, collected July 28. This

European species was first recorded from this country by the writer about three years ago, the localities being in New Hampshire and

Massachusetts.

Panzeria radicum (Fabricius).

Musca radicum Fabricius, Systema Entom., p. 778, 1775. *Nemoraa radicum* Schiner, Fauna Austriaca, Dipt., 1, p. 452, 1862. *Panzeria radicum* Coquillett, Revision Tachinidae, p. 88, 1897.

Fox Point, Alaska: A single specimen, collected July 28. Also a European species, first reported from this country at the same time is the preceding species. It has heretofore been recorded as occurring from New Hampshire, southward to the District of Columbia, westward to Texas and northward to British Columbia.

Paraphyto borealis sp. no v.

Black, the anterior portion of the cheeks and lower part of sides of face reddish brown, median depression sometimes of the same color; front of male at narrowest point narrower than distance between the posterior ocelli, in the female one and one-half times as wide as either eye, the sides and face dark gray pruinose, a dark brownish spot on each side of face near lower end of fronttlvisible only in certain lights, frontal bristles not descending to base of second antennal joint, two pairs of orbital bristles in the female, wanting in the male, antennae reaching lowest fourth of face, the third joint nearly one and one-half times as long as the second, arista thickened on the basal sixth, pubescent, the longest pubescence slightly longer than the greatest diameter of the arista; vibrissae situated slightly above the oral margin, two or three bristles above each, proboscis rigid and rather slender, the labella small; mesonotum thinly gray pruinose, marked with three black, polished vittae, four dorsocentral, postsutural macrochaetae and three sternopleural; abdomen somewhat polished, anterior portion of the second, third, and fourth segments gray pruinose, the first three segments bearing marginal, the second and third also with discal macrochaetae, hypopygium uniformly covered with hairs; wings hyaline, the base pale brownish, anterior veins indistinctly bordered with brown, calypteres white. Length 9 mm. A specimen of each sex, collected July 28.

Habitat.—Fox Point, Alaska. *Type.*—Cat. no. 5242, U. S. National Museum. Closely related to *gillettei,* but in that species the eyes of the male are at least twice as wide apart as the distance between the two posterior ocelli, the hairs of the hypopygium are arranged in transverse bands widely separated by bare intervals, there are no brown spots on upper part of the face, and the length is from 12 to 14 mm.

Echinomyia algens (Wiedemann).

Tachina algens Wiedemann, Ausser. Zweif. Insekten, 11, p. 285, 1830. *Echinomyia algens* Coquillett, Revision Tachinidae, p. 144, 1897.

Fox Point, Alaska: A single specimen, collected July 28. This species was originally described from North America, without any mention of a more precise locality. It has been reported as occurring from Canada to New York and westward to British Columbia and California.

Family SARCOPHAGUS.

Cynomyia cadaverina Desvoidy.

Cynomyia cadaverina Desvoidy, Essai Myod., p. 365, 1830. *Cynomyia americana* Hough, Entom. News, p. 105, 1898.

Sitka, Alaska: A single specimen, collected June 16. This species was originally described from "Carolina," and has been reported as occurring from Canada to Georgia, and westward to Colorado.

Cynomyia mortisequa (Kirby).

Musca mortisequa Kirby, Fauna Bor.-Amer., iv, p. 317, 1837. *Cynomyia hirta* Hough, Entom. News, p. 166, 1898.

Kukak Bay, July 4; Popof Island, July 8; Kadiak, Alaska, July 20: Ten.specimens. Originally described from British America, latitude 650. It has already been reported from Alaska.

Calliphora vomitoria (Linn£).

Musca vomitoria Linne, Fauna Suecica, p. 1831, 1761. *Calliphora vomitoria* Schiner, Fauna Austr., Dipt., 1, p. 584, 1862.

Sitka, June 16; Kukak Bay, July 1; Popof Island, July 9 and 10; Saldovia, Alaska, July 21: Seven specimens. A European species reported as occurring in this country over twenty years ago. It has also been recorded from Alaska, and the U. S. National Museum contains a specimen collected as far southward as Alabama.

Calliphora viridescens Desvoidy.

Calliphora viridescens Desvoidy, Essai Myod., p. 437, 1830.

Lowe Inlet, British Columbia, June 3; Metlakahtla, June 4; Yakutat, June 21; Virgin Bay, June 26; Kukak Bay, July 4; Kadiak, July 20; Saldovia, July 21; Juneau, Alaska, July 25: Fourteen specimens. Originally described from 'Carolina '; it is known to occur over the greater portion of this country.

Lucilia caesar (Linne).

Musca caesar Linne, Fauna Suecica, p. 1828, 1761. *Lucilia casar* Schiner, Fauna Austriaca, Dipt., 1, p. 590, 1862.

Lowe Inlet, British Columbia; Kukak Bay, July 4; Popof Island, July 8; Kadiak, Alaska, July 20: Ten specimens. A European species first recorded from this country about sixty years ago, and now occurring in almost every part of North America.

Phormia terraenovae Desvoidy.

Phormia terranova Desvoidy, Essai Myod., p. 467,1830.—Hough, Zool. Bulletin, p. 289, 1899.

Juneau, July 25; Fox Point, Alaska, July 28: Six specimens. Originally described from Newfoundland, but occurring over the greater part of North America.

Graphomyia maculata (Scopoli).

Musca maculata Scopoli, Entom. Carniolica, p. 326, 1763.

Graphomyia maculata Schiner, Fauna Austriaca, Dipt., I, p. 582, 1862.

Graphomyia americana Desvoidy, Essai Myod., p. 404, 1830.

Popof Island, Alaska: A single specimen, collected July 10. A European species, first reported from this country about seventy years ago. It has been recorded from Greenland, and specimens are in the National Museum from Virginia and Kansas.

Mesembrina latreillei Desvoidy.

Mesembrina latreillei Desvoidy, Essai Myod., p. 401, 1830.

Kukak Bay, July 4; Kadiak, July 20; Saldovia, July 21, Juneau, Alaska, July 25: Four specimens. This species was originally described from Nova Scotia, and its most southern recorded limit is Pennsylvania.

Myospila meditabunda (Fabricius).

Musca meditabunda Fabricius, Species Insect., 11, p. 444, 1781.

Myospila meditabunda Schiner, Fauna Austriaca, Dipt., 1, p. 598, 1862.

Cyrtomura 4-signata Thomson, Kongliga Sven. Fregatten Eugenies Resa, p. 549, 1868.

Metlakahtla, June 4; Yakutat, Alaska, June 21: Three specimens. A European species, first reported as occurring in this country about thirty-six years ago.

Hyetodesia varipes sp. nov.

Male: Black, the apex of scutellum reddish yellow, apices of front femora and whole of their tibiae yellowish brown, apices of middle femora, the whole of their tibiae, also the hind femora and tibiae, yellow, halteres light yellow; hairs of eyes long and dense, frontal orbits white pruinose, contiguous a short distance in front of the ocelli, or narrowly separated, antennae reaching about two-thirds of distance to oral margin, the third joint less than twice as long as the second, arista long plumose, the longest hairs about three times as long as greatest diameter of the arista; mesonotum somewhat polished, rather thinly light gray pruinose, marked with four black vittae; four pairs of postsutural dorsocentral bristles, no acrostichals in front of the suture,

Family MUSCHXffi.

Family Anthomyiidje. praesutural intra-alar bristle longer than the adjacent supra-alar, sternopleurals i + 2; abdomen yellowish gray pruinose and with darker, olivaceous, reflecting spots; front tibiae destitute of bristles except at the apices, middle femora ciliate with bristles on the basal two-thirds of the under side, middle tibiae each bearing three bristles on the posterior side of about their median third, hind femora ciliate the entire length of their anterior-under side and with two bristles on the median third, or penultimate fourth, of their posterior-under side, hind tibiae each bearing from two to four short bristles on the inner-anterior side, two or three longer ones on the outer-anterior side, all on the median third of the tibia, also one on the outer side near three-fourths of the length of the tibia; front pulvilli as long as the last tarsal joint; wings hyaline, tinged with yellowish brown at base and along the anterior half, hind crossvein strongly sinuous, small and hind crossveins bordered with brown, third and fourth veins diverging, costal spine shorter than the small crossvein, calypteres yellowish.

Female: Same as the male with these exceptions: Middle femora and sometimes the front ones and their tibiae, yel-

low; hairs of eyes rather sparse, front nearly twice as wide as either eye, destitute of a pair of praeocellar bristles, a dark, changeable spot on upper part of sides of face, front pulvilli much shorter than the last tarsal joint. Length, 8 to 10 mm. Two males and three females.

Habitat.—Sitka, June 16; Kadiak, June 20; Yakutat, June 21; Popof Island, Alaska, July 14. *Type.*—Cat. no. 5243, U. S. National Museum.

Hyetodesia lucorum (Fallen).

Muse a lucorum Fallen, Diptera Suec., Muscidse, p. 55, 1820.

Aricia lucorum Schiner, Fauna Austr., Diptera, 1, p. 600, 1862.

Kukak Bay, July 4; Popof Island, July 8 to 12; Kadiak, Alaska, July 20: Ten specimens, of both sexes. A European species first reported from this country by Mr. P. Stein about two years ago, recorded as occurring in Massachusetts, Pennsylvania, Kansas, and Idaho.

Hyetodesia brunneinervis (Stein).

Aricia brunneinervis Stein, Berliner Ent. Zeitsch., p. 183, 1898.

Berg Bay, June 10; Sitka, June 16; Yakutat, June 21; Virgin Bay, June 26; Kukak Bay, July 4; Popof Island, July 9 to 12; Kadiak, July 20; Saldovia, Alaska, July 21: Forty-seven specimens. Originally described from Idaho.

Hyetodesia septentrionalis (Stein).

Aricia septentrionalis Stein, Berliner Ent. Zeitsch., p. 184, 1898.

Sitka, June 16; Virgin Bay, June 21; Kukak Bay, July 4; Popof Island, July 8 to 14; Kadiak, July 20; Saldovia, Alaska, July 21: Fifty-five specimens of both sexes. The type locality of this species is Alaska.

Hyetodesia villicrura sp. nov.

Male: Black, the halteres brown; hair of eyes long and densey frontal vitta at narrowest point narrower than the lowest ocellus, antennae three-fourths as long as the face, the third joint one and onehalf times as long as the second, a white pruinose spot between bases of antennae, arista long pubescent, the longest slightly more than greatest diameter of the arista; mesonotum polished, not gray pruinose except on the sides, four pairs of postsutural dorsocentral bristles, sternopleurals 1 + 2;

abdomen narrowly subovate, slightly over twice as long as wide, polished, thinly olive gray pruinose, the greater portion of the first segment and a dorsal, indistinct, subtriangular spot on the second and third, blackish, hypopygium only slightly projecting; front tibiae short haired on the lower half of its inner side, interspersed with about three long and four shorter bristly hairs; middle femora densely long haired on the basal two-thirds of the under side, their tibiae each bearing about five bristles along the outer-posterior side and with about six bristles and a few shorter bristly hairs on the lower two-thirds of the inner-posterior side; hind femora densely long haired on the under side, their tibia; with similar hairs along the inner, anterior-inner, and posterior-inner sides, the outer side ciliate with rather short bristly hairs interspersed with about four longer bristles on the lower two-thirds; wings pale brownish, changing into grayish hyaline along the hind margin, nearly wholly hyaline in the younger specimens, costal spine minute, third and fourth veins diverging, hind crossvein almost straight; calypteres yellowish white, the lower extending far beyond the upper.

Female: Differs from the male as follows: Halteres yellow, eyes bare, front at narrowest point slightly narrower than either eye, a praeocellar, cruciate pair of bristles present; mesonotum opaque, yellowish gray pruinose; abdomen subovate, slightly polished, grayish yellow pruinose, unmarked; front tibiae destitute of bristles except at the apices, middle femora sparsely short haired on the under side, their tibiae pubescent on the inner-posterior side but with two or three bristles on lower half of the outer-anterior side; hind femora bearing five or six bristles on the apical half of the underside, and sometimes with a few long hairs on the basal portion; hind tibiae pubescent, each bearing about four bristles on the median two-fourths of the anterior-inner side, two or three on median third of the outer-anterior side, and about five on the lower two-thirds of the outer-posterior side; wings hyaline, strongly tinged with yel-

low at the base. Length, 6 to 8 mm. Thirty males and thirty-one females. *Habitat.*—Yakutat, June 21; Kukak Bay, July 4; Popof Island, July 8 to 15; Kadiak, July 20; Saldovia, Alaska, July 21. *Type.*—Cat. no. 5244, U. S. National Museum.

Lasiops frenata (Holmgren.) *Aricia frenata* Holmgren, Ofversigt Vetans.-Akad. Forh., p. 103, 1872.

Muir Inlet, Alaska: A male specimen, collected June 12. Originally described from Greenland.

Lasiops hirsutula (Zetterstedt).
Anthomyza hirsutula Zetterstedt, Insecta Lapp., p. 673, 1840.
Aricia hirsutula Zetterstedt, Diptera Scand., IV, p. 1494, 1845.
Popof Island, Alaska: Two male specimens, taken July 13 and 15. A European species, not before reported as occurring on this Continent.

Lasiops calvicrura sp. nov.
Male: Black, the halteres light yellow; hairs of eyes rather long and quite dense, frontal vitta at narrowest point narrower than the lowest ocellus, antennae two-thirds as long as the face, the third joint twice as long as the second, arista rather long pubescent, the longest about equal to greatest diameter of the arista; mesonotum polished, two indistinct gray pruinose vittae in front of the suture, four pairs of postsutural dorsocentral bristles, sternopleurals 1 + 2; abdomen less than twice as long as broad, subelliptical, yellowish gray pruinose and with darker, olivaceous reflecting spots, the greater part of the first segment and a pair of indistinct, subtriangular spots on the second, black, hypopygium projecting very slightly; front tibiae destitute of bristles, middle femora ciliate with bristles on the entire length of the under side, their tibiae each bearing a bristle near the middle of the anterior-outer side and with four on the median two-fourths of the posterior-outer side; hind femora ciliate the entire length of the anterior-under and posterior-under sides with bristles which become gradually" shorter toward each end of the femur; hind tibiae short pubescent, each bearing three bristles on about the median third

of the anterior-inner side and with four on the median two-fourths of the anterior-outer side; wings pale brownish, changing into grayish hyaline along the hind margin and in the discal cell, third and fourth veins diverging, hind crossvein slightly sinuous, costal spine not longer than the small crossvein, calypteres yellow, the lower ones projecting far beyond the upper.

Female: Differs from the male as follows: Eyes bare, front at narrowest part almost twice as wide as either eye, no praeocellar bristles, third joint of antennae scarcely one and one-half times as long as the second, arista short pubescent, the longest scarcely half the length of greatest diameter of the arista, mesonotum opaque, bluish gray pruinose, marked with five dark brown vittae, sternopleurals i + i, abdomen broadly subelliptical, about one and one-third times as long as wide, densely bluish gray pruinose, a pair of dark brown spots along the hind margins of the second and third segments, middle tibiae each bearing only two bristles, situated on the median third of the posterior side, besides those at the tip, hind femora bearing a few rather short hairs on the under side of its basal half and with five bristles on the apical half; wings hyaline. Length, 6 to 7 mm. Two males and one female, collected July 9, 10, and 12. *Habitat.*—Popof Island, Alaska. *Type.*—Cat. no. 5245, U. S. National Museum.

Limnophora nobilis Stein.
Umnophora nobilis Stein, Berliner Ent. Zeitsch., p. 207, 1898.
Muir Inlet, June 12; Sitka, June 16; Popof Island, July 8 to 12; Saldovia, Alaska, July 21: Twenty-seven specimens. Originally described from Alaska.

Coenosia fuscopunctata Macquart.
Ccenosia fuscopunctata Macquart, Dipteres Exot., 4 Suppl., p. 270, 1849.
Canosia ovata Stein, Berliner Ent. Zeitsch., p. 263, 1898.
Popof Island, July 11; Saldovia, Alaska, July 21: Two specimens. Originally described from North America, without any indication of the exact locality; it has been reported as occurring from

New Hampshire to Florida, and westward to Illinois.

Coenosia lata Walker.

Canosia lata Walker, Insecta Saund., Diptera, p. 368, 1856.

Canosia canescens Stein, Berliner Ent. Zeitsch., p. 265, 1898.

Lowe Inlet, British Columbia; Muir Inlet, June 12; Virgin Bay, June 26; Kukak Bay, July 4; Popof Island, July 8 to 14; Saldovia, Alaska, July 21: Twenty specimens. Originally described from the United States, without mention of any more definite locality. It has been recorded from the same region as the preceding species, except that its western limits are stated to be Kansas and South Dakota.

Ccenosia albifrons (Zetterstedt).

Aricia albifrons Zetterstedt, Dipt. Scand.,v11i, p. 3301, 1849.

Muir Inlet, June 11 and 12; Popof Island, July 10; Saldovia, Alaska, July 21: Eight specimens. A European species, first recorded from this country about two years ago by Mr. P. Stein, of Genthin, Germany, whose specimens were collected in Massachusetts.

Homalomyia flavivaria sp. nov.

Male: Black, the halteres, except their bases, and a pair of large spots on the second and third abdominal segments, light yellow, the spots on the second segment subquadrate, those on the third subtriangular, also usually a yellow spot at the anterior angles of the fourth segment; frontal orbits whitish pruinose, in immature specimens contiguous for a considerable distance on the median portion, but rather widely separated in mature ones, antennae almost as long as the face, the third joint one and one-half times as long as the second; mesonotum slightly polished, the sides and pleura light gray pruinose, three pairs of postsutural dorsocentral bristles, sternopleurals 1-f-I; abdomen nearly linear but sometimes widening posteriorly, very thinly gray pruinose; coxae destitute of stout spines, front tibiae without bristles except at apices, middle femora gradually thickening toward the middle, then slightly narrowing, with a small, rounded prominence at two-thirds the length of the under

side, which is densely covered with short bristles, beyond this the femur is rather suddenly narrowed, and continues so to the apex, the under-posterior side ciliate with long bristles except on the apical fourth, on the anterior-under side bearing two stout spines at one-fourth its length, beyond which it is ciliate with rather long bristles to the prominence, the basal half of the narrowed apical portion bare, the apical half ciliate with about six very short bristles, middle tibiae each bearing a small, rounded process at one-third of its inner side, the apical half considerably thickened and with rather long pubescence on the inner side, bearing a pair of bristles at three-fourths its length, one on the anterior and the other on the posterior side; hind femora sparsely ciliate with rather short bristles on the basal two-thirds of the anterior-under side, the posterior-under side bare; hind tibiae each bearing two bristles on the penultimate fifth of the anterior-inner side, one below middle of anterior side, and two on apical half of the anterior-outer side; wings hyaline, fourth vein usually slightly curving toward the third at its apex, calypteres yellowish, the upper projecting beyond the lower.

Female: Abdomen yellow, hind margins of the first three segments black, front one and one-half times as wide as either eye, two pairs of orbital bristles, no praeocellar bristles, middle legs simple, middle femora destitute of spines, the anterior-under and posterior-undersides sparsely ciliate with short bristles, otherwise as in the male. Length, 4 to 5. 5 mm. Fifteen males and eight females. *Habitat.*—Metlakahtla, June 4; Berg Bay, June 10; Sitka, June 16; Yakutat, June 21; Virgin Bay, June 26; Kukak Bay, July 4; Popof Island, Alaska, July 10 to 12. *Type.*—Cat. no. 5246, U. S. National Museum.

Homalomyia flavibasis Stein.

Ifomalomyia flavibasis STE.m, Berliner Ent. Zeitsch., p. 171, 1898.

Sitka, June 16; Yakutat, June 21; Virgin Bay, June 26; Popof Island, July 10 and 12; Juneau, Alaska, July 25: Eleven specimens. The type locality of this

species is Illinois.

Hydrophoria ambigua (Fallen).

Musca ambigua Fallen, Diptera Sueciae, Muscidae, p. 56, 1820.

Aricia ambigua Zetterstedt, Dipt. Scand., XII, p. 4719, 1855.

Metlakahtla, Alaska: A single specimen, collected June 4. This is also a European species, recorded from Massachusetts and Illinois about two years ago, by Mr. Stein.

Anthomyia radicum (Linn6).

Musca radicum Linne, Fauna Suecica, p. 1840, 1761. *Anthomyia radicum* Schiner, Fauna Austriaca, Diptera, I, p. 645, 1862.

Yakutat, Alaska: A specimen of each sex, collected June 21. This

European species was first reported from this country about nineteen years ago, by Mr. R. H. Meade, of Bradford, England. It has been recorded from Canada to Pennsylvania, westward to Idaho.

Anthomyia mystacea sp. nov.

Black, the halteres yellow; front in profile slightly concave, frontal vitta at narrowest part narrower than the lowest ocellus, face strongly concave, oral margin projecting farther forward than the front, vibrissae not longer than the adjacent bristles; extending obliquely downward and backward from near each vibrissa are several irregular, dense rows of long, upwardly curving bristly hairs, the rows almost equalling length of face, lower part of front projecting more than length of third antennal joint in front of the eyes, antennae nearly three-fourths as long as the face, the third joint one and one-half times as long as the second, proboscis nearly as long as height of head, the labellavery small; mesonotum slightly polished, two median vittae in front of the suture, the lateral margins in front of wings and the pleura, gray pruinose, three pairs of postsutural dorsocentral bristles; abdomen depressed, elongate-ellipsoidal, almost one and one-half times as long as broad, subopaque, dark gray pruinose, a broad dorsal vitta and very narrow bases of the segments, black; hypopygium only slightly projecting, opaque, gray pruinose; venter, especially along the sides, densely covered with rather long hairs; middle femora covered on the anterior-under side with short bristles, on the posterior-under side with long bristly hairs, becoming shorter toward apices of the femora; middle tibiae each bearing a bristle at three-fourths the length of the outer-anterior side, three on lower half of outer-posterior side and two below middle of inner-posterior side; hind femora on the anteriorunder side ciliate with long bristles and hairs, the posterior-under side ciliate with shorter bristles which are much shorter on the apical third; hind tibiae each bearing a bristle below the middle of the inner-anterior side, the outer-anterior side ciliate with about nine rather short bristles on about the median three-fifths, the outer-posterior side ciliate with about three long and three shorter bristles on about the median third; wings hyaline, costal vein pubescent, third and fourth veins slightly converging, hind crossvein very sinuate, calypteres white; length, 6 mm. A male specimen, collected July 28. *Habitat.*—Juneau, Alaska. *Type.*—Cat. no. 5247, U. S. National Museum.

Hylemyia alcathoe (Walker).

Anthomyia alcathoe Walker, List Dipt. Ins. Britisli Museum, iv, p. 937, 1849. *Hylemyia flavicaudata* Bigot, Annates Soc. Ent. France, p. 299, 1884. *Hylemyia strigata* Stein, Berliner Ent. Zeitsch., p. 211, 1898.

Sitka, Alaska: Nine specimens, collected June 16. Originally described from Nova Scotia, and has been recorded from Idaho and Washington. The U. S. National Museum also possesses specimens collected at Franconia, New Hampshire, by Mrs. Annie T. Slosson.

Hylemyia variata (Fallen).

Musca variata Fallen, Dipt. Sueciae, Muscidse, p. 59, 1820.—Schiner, Fauna Austriaca, Dipt., 1, p. 628, 1862.

Popof Island, Alaska: Six specimens, collected July 8 to 12. A European species, first reported from this country about two years ago by Mr. P. Stein, who recorded it as occurring from Canada to Virginia, westward to Idaho.

Hylemyia marginata Stein.

Hylemyia marginata Stein, Berliner Ent. Zeitsch., p. 221, 1898.

Sitka, Alaska: A male specimen, collected June 16. The type locality of this species is Colorado.

Hylemyia linearis Stein.

Hylemyia linearis Stein, Berliner Ent. Zeitsch., p. 219, 1898.

Kukak Bay, Alaska: Two male specimens, collected July 4. This species was originally described from Minnesota.

Hylemyia spiniventris sp. nov.

Male: Black, the halteres yellow; frontal vitta at narrowest part slightly wider than the lowest ocellus, antennae about five-sixths as long as the face, the third joint only slightly longer than the second, longest hairs of arista almost twice as long as greatest diameter of the arista, proboscis slightly longer than height of head, very slender, the label la very small; mesonotum slightly polished, two median vittae in front of the suture, the lateral margins in front of the wings, and the pleura, grayish pruinose, three pairs of postsutural dorsocentral bristles, sternopleurals 1-f 2; abdomen somewhat depressed, almost linear, subopaque, yellowish gray pruinose and with darker, olivaceous reflecting spots, hairs of venter becoming gradually longer toward its apex, the plate on the fifth ventral segment beset along each outer edge with about eight stout, rather short, inwardly curving spines, near the apex of the plate with a transverse pair of clusters of rather long' bristles and hairs; front tibiae each bearing two bristles below the middle of the posterior side and with three below middle of outer side; middle femora ciliate with bristles along the anterior-under and posterior-under sides, middle tibiae each bearing two bristles on the outer-anterior side, three on the posterior-outer side, and two or three on the inner-posterior side, all on about the median third of the tibia; hind femora sparsely ciliate with long bristles on the anterior-under side and basal half of the posterior-under side, the apical half of the latter side ciliate with short bristles; hind tibiae each bearing three bristles on the inner-anterior side, four on the outer-anterior side, five on the outer-posterior side, and about four short ones

on the basal half of the posterior side; wings dark brown at base, the remainder pale brown, changing into grayish hyaline along the hind margin, costal vein distinctly spined to apex of first vein, costal spine slightly longer than the small crossvein, hind crossvein strongly sinuate, calypteres yellow.

Female: Front at narrowest point almost one and one-half times as wide as either eye, a pair of cruciate praaocellar bristles; mesonotum opaque yellowish gray pruinose, marked with five indistinct brown vittae, abdomen elongate oval, fifth ventral segment destitute of spines and of long bristles; middle femora each bearing one long bristle on the basal fifth of the anterior-under side and with short ones on the remainder, with three long ones on the basal half of the posteriorunder side and with short ones on the apical half; hind tibiae destitute of bristles on the posterior side; wings grayish hyaline, yellow in the costal cell, the veins largely yellow, otherwise as in the male. Length, 6 to 8 mm. Two pairs, taken in coition, July 10.

Habitat.—Popof Island, Alaska. *Type.*—Cat. no. 5248, U. S. National Museum.

Hylemyia simpla sp. nov.

Black, the halteres yellow, lower part of front yellowish brown; frontal orbits contiguous for a short distance, antennae nearly as long as the face, the third joint only slightly longer than the second, longest hairs of arista scarcely longer than greatest diameter of the arista; proboscis short and rather slender, label la large; mesonotum subopaque, thinly dark grayish pruinose, the sides in front of wings light gray pruinose, three pairs of postsutural dorsocentral bristles, sternopleurals 1 4-2; abdomen depressed, nearly linear, dark gray pruinose, the first segment and a median vitta, black, hairs of venter slightly in'creasing in length toward its apex, hypopygium gray pruinose, destitute of long bristles on its apical portion; front tibiae each bearing a bristle near the middle of its inner-posterior side, the bristle at apex of inner side sharppointed; middle femora on the anterior-under side and apical half of the posterior-under side ciliate with rather short bristles, on the basal half of the posterior-under side with very long ones; middle tibiae each bearing one bristle on the inner-anterior side, one on the outer-anterior, one on the outer-posterior, and two on the innerposterior side, all near the middle of the tibia; hind femora sparsely ciliate on the anterior-under side with rather long bristles, the posterior-under side with very short ones and near the apex with two or three rather long ones; hind tibiae each bearing about six rather short bristles on the anterior-inner side, five on the anterior-outer side, three long ones on the outer side, the inner-posterior side ciliate with rather short ones on the basal three-fourths; wings hyaline, costal vein ciliate with very short spines, costal spine much longer than the small crossvein, hind crossvein almost straight, calypteres yellowish; length, 5 mm. A male specimen, collected June 16.

Habitat.—Sitka, Alaska. *Type.*—Cat. no. 5249, U. S. National Museum.

Hylemyia fabricii (Holmgren).

Aricia fabricii Holmgren, Ofversigt Vetan.-Akad. Forh., p. Ioi, 1872.

Kukak Bay, July 4; Popof Island, Alaska, July 9 to 11: Thirteen specimens of both sexes. Originally described from Greenland, and the U. S. National Museum contains a male specimen collected at Franconia, New Hampshire, by Mrs. Annie T. Slosson. The two long ribbon-like appendages of the hypopygium are visible only when the hypopygium is disengaged.

Pegomyia costalis Stein.

Pegomyia costalis Stein, Berliner Ent. Zeitsch., p. 243, 1898.

Kukak Bay, July 4; Saldovia, Alaska, July 21: Two specimens. The type locality of this species is South Dakota.

Phorbia pretiosa (Walker).

Ariphia pretiosa Walker, List Dipt. Ins. British Museum, iv, p. 965, 1849.

Lowe Inlet, British Columbia, June 3; Sitka, June 16; Yakutat, June 21; Juneau, Alaska, July 25: Ten specimens. Originally described from the Albany River, British America.

Phorbia biciliata sp. nov.

Male: Black, the halteres yellow, lower part of front yellowish brown; frontal orbits unusually broad, contiguous for a considerable distance, only three or four pairs of very short front bristles, the ocellar bristles not longer than the adjoining hairs, antennae three-fourths as long as the face, the third joint scarcely one and one-half times as long as the second, arista with a very short pubescence, proboscis rather slender, labella small; thorax, scutellum, and abdomen whitish pruinose, unmarked, abdomen depressed, very elongate oval, hairs of venter sparse and of nearly a uniform length, hypopygium unusually large, its two segments together much longer than the preceding segment, the two lamellae of the fifth ventral segment very large, each bearing a row of about four short spines at the apex; front tibiae each bearing a bristle near middle of the posterior side, the bristle at apex of inner side slender and sharp pointed; middle femora ciliate on the anterior-under and posterior-under sides with rather short bristles, middle tibiae each bearing two bristles on the median third of the outer-posterior side and with one below middle of the inner-posterior side; hind femora ciliate on the anterior-under and posterior-under sides with bristles which are very short on the bases of the femora but gradually become rather long toward the apices; hind tibiae ciliate with rather short bristles along the entire length of the inner-anterior side, with five or six rather short bristles on the median two-fourths of the outer-anterior side, with three bristles which are successively longer, located at the first, second and third fifths of the outer side, the inner-posterior side ciliate with rather short, downwardly curving bristles on nearly its entire length; wings whitish hyaline, costal vein not spined, costal spine minute, hind crossvein slightly curved; calypteres white.

Female: Front at narrowest point slightly wider than either eye, ocellar and frontal bristles stout, a pair of praeocellar bristles; front tibiaa destitute of bristles except at the apices, middle tibiae each with one bristle below

middle of outer-anterior side and one near middle of outer-posterior side; hind tibiae each bearing about three bristles below middle of the inner-anterior side, two on median third of the outer-anterior side, and three on the outer-posterior side, otherwise nearly as in the male. Length, 3 mm. A specimen of each sex, collected June 10.

Habitat.—Berg Bay, Alaska. *Type.*—Cat. no. 5250, U. S. National Museum.

Hylephila silvestris (Fallen).

Musca silvestris Fallen, Diptera Sueciae, Muscidae, p. 70, 1820.

Aricia silvestris Zetterstedt, Dipt. Scand., iv, p. 1527, 1845.

Anthomyza murina Zetterstedt, Insecta Lappon., p. 682, 1840.

Aricia decrepita Zetterstedt, Dipt. Scand., iv, p. 1454, 1845.

Kukak Bay, July 4; Popof Island, July 10; Kadiak, Alaska, July 20: Thirteen specimens, of both sexes. A European species, now for the first time reported from this Continent. The synonymy is according to Mr. P. Stein, who made an examination of Zetterstedt's types. This examination revealed the fact that in the cases of both *murina* and *decrepita,* Zetterstedt had mistaken the females for males.

Chirosia glauca sp. nov.

Male: Black, the arista, except the basal fourth, and the halteres yellow, front at narrowest point almost as wide as either eye, a pair of small, cruciate praeocellar bristles; antennae nearly as long as the face, the third joint one and one-half times as long as the second, proboscis short and rather robust, palpi each bearing about four rather long bristles; body opaque, bluish gray pruinose, about four irregular pairs of praesutural acrostichal bristles, sternopleurals four, the lower two scarcely stouter than bristly hairs; abdomen depressed, elongateellipsoidal, hypopygium unusually large, nearly concealed beneath the abdomen; front tibiae destitute of bristles, front pulvilli about one-half as long as the last tarsal joint, middle femora on under side sparsely covered with rather short bristles, middle tibiae each bearing a short bristle at two-thirds the length of the inner-anterior side and with one near middle of the outer-posterior side; hind femora ciliate with long bristles on the anterior-under side and with rather short ones on the basal half of the posterior-under side; hind tibiae each bearing two short bristles on lower half of the inner-anterior side, three rather long ones on the outer-anterior and four on the outer-posterior sides; wings hyaline, costal vein ciliate with very short spines, costal spine slightly longer than the small crossvein; calypteres yellowish white; length 4.5 mm. A male specimen, collected June 8. *Habitat.*—Farragut Bay, Alaska. *Type.* —Cat. no. 5251, U. S. National Museum.

Chirosia thinobia (Thomson).
Scatophaga thinobia Thomson, Kongliga Svenska Fregatt. Engenies Resa, p. 563. 1868.
Metlakahtla, June 4; Sitka, June 16; Saldovia, Alaska, July 21: Twelve specimens. Originally described from California.

Fucellia fucorum (Fallen).
Scatomyza fucorum Fallen, Diptera Sueciae, Scatomyzidae, p. 5, 1819.
Fucellia fucorum Schiner, Fauna Austriaca, Dipt., 11, p. 15, 1864.
Sitka, June 16; Kukak Bay, July 4; Popof Island, July 8; Saldovia, Alaska, July 21: Twenty-eight specimens. A European species, first reported from this country about sixty years ago. It is a maritime species, reported as occurring from Greenland to Florida, and also in the Bering Islands.

Family SCATOPHAGIDiE.
Scatophaga stercoraria (Linne).
Musca stercoraria Linne, Fauna Suecica, p. 1861, 1761. *Scatophaga stercoraria* Schiner, Fauna Austriaca, Dipt., 11, p. 18, 1864.
Kadiak, July 20; Juneau, Alaska, July 25: Ten specimens. Originally described from Europe, but at present almost cosmopolitan.

Scatophaga furcata (Say).
Pyropa furcata Say, Journal Acad. Nat. Sciences Philadelphia, p. 98, 1823. *Scatophaga squalida* Meigen, System. Besch. Eur. Zweif. Ins., v, p. 252, 1826.
Lowe Inlet, British Columbia, June 3; Metlakahtla, June 4; Sitka, June 16;

Popof Island, July 11 to 14; Kadiak, Alaska, July 20: Nine specimens. This species was originally described from Missouri, but occurs over the greater portion of North America, ranging Proc. Wash. Acad. Sci., November, 1900. from Greenland and Alaska to Georgia and Texas. It also occurs in Europe, and is one of the very few species described in this country before it was in Europe.

Scatophaga intermedia Walker.
Scatophaga intermedia Walker, List Dipt. Inst. Brit. Museum, iv, p. 980, 1849.
Muir Inlet, Alaska: A single specimen, collected June 11. The type locality is Nova Scotia. This species has also been recorded from New Hampshire and from Bering Islands; specimens are in the U. S. National Museum from Maine and Massachusetts.

Scatophaga suilla (Fabricius).
Muse a suilla Fabricius, Entomol. Syst. , iv, p. 343, 1794. *Scatophaga spurca* Meigen, System. Besch. Eur. Zweif. Ins., v, p. 250, 1826.
Sitka, June 16; Virgin Bay, June 26; Popof Island, July 10 to 13; Kadiak, Alaska, July 20: Twelve specimens. A European species not before recorded from this Continent. The U. S. National Museum contains specimens from New Hampshire, Canada, Washington, and Colorado.

Scatophaga islandica Becker.
Scatophaga islandica Becker, Berliner Ent. Zeitsch., p. 175, 1894.
Berg Bay, June 10; Yakutat, June 21; Popof Island, July 8 to 11; Kadiak, Alaska, July 20: Fifteen specimens. Originally described from Iceland and Labrador; it has also been reported from Bering Islands.

Scatophaga frigida sp. nov.
Male and female: Black, the frontal vittae yellowish red, cheeks and sides of face pale yellow, arista beyond the thickened basal part, palpi, and halteres yellow, tibiae reddish yellow; third joint of antennae twice as long as the second, arista short plumose on the antepenultimate fourth, the longest hairs one and one-half times as long as greatest diameter of arista; under side of palpi rather thickly beset with long yellowish white

bristly hairs, the upper side with very short, the apices with long black bristles; body opaque, bluish gray pruinose, mesonotum marked with four blackish brown vittae, its bristles and sparse, father short hairs black; hairs of pleura long and abundant, those of the mesopleura chiefly black, of the sternopleura yellow, pteropleura bare; abdomen densely covered with long hairs, those on the dorsum chiefly black, on the venter yellow; femora, except upper side of the puddle ones, rather densely covered with long black and yellow hairs, tibiae more sparsely covered with long black ones, hind and middle femora destitute of bristles, middle tibial each with two bristles on the anterior and two on the posterior side, hind tibiae each with two or three on the anterior and two on the posterior side besides those at the apices; wings pale yellowish gray, changing to hyaline along the hind margin, crossveins not clouded with brown; calypteres white; length 8 to 10 mm. Two males and one female.
Habitat.—Kukak Bay, July 4; Popof Island, Alaska, July 9. *Type.*—Cat. no. 5252, U. S. National Museum.
The U. S. National Museum also possesses a male specimen collected at Port Chester, Alaska, by Professor H. F. Wickham.

Pogonota kincaJdi sp. nov.
Male: Black, the front on lower part, in the middle almost reaching the ocellar triangle, face, cheeks, antennae, palpi, halteres, anterior portion of front coxae, and the legs, yellow; third joint of antennae three times as long as the second, arista bare, vibrissae and the bristles and hairs along lower side of head yellow, hairs on lower side of occiput extremely sparse; a velvet-black, H-shaped spot near center of front; body slightly polished, thinly grayish pruinose, hairs on dorsum of abdomen very short except a fringe of long black ones near hind margins of the fourth, fifth, and sixth segments; end lamellae of hypopygium each slightly longer than wide, directed upward, the apex fringed with long pale yellow hairs which curve over the back; in front of the hypopygium is a pair of ventral processes

which, near the middle of the anterior side, send forth an anteriorly directed, compressed, obliquely truncated lobe, beyond which the main process is strongly bent backward, but curves slightly forward toward its apex; front femora greatly swollen, considerably narrowed toward the apex of the under side, bearing many very short, black bristles on the under side of the thickened portion and on the inner side of the front tibiae; wings whitish hyaline, a pale brownish vitta in the middle, most pronounced beyond the small crossvein, second basal cell slightly widening toward the apex, crossvein at base of discal cell almost perpendicular, hairs along the costa extremely short; calypteres whitish.

Female: Differs from the male as follows: Yellow of front extends above lowest ocellus, third joint of antennae black, proboscis yellow, its apex brown, front coxae wholly yellow, vibrissae and two adjacent bristles black, no velvet-black mark near center of front, abdomen not pruinose, highly polished, destitute of long hairs and of ventral processes, depressed at base, strongly compressed at apex, ovipositor nearly linear, about three times as long as greatest width, tapering to a point at apex, front femora only slightly thickened, no black bristles on their under sides nor on inner sides of the front tibiae; wings hyaline, unmarked. Length, 5 mm. A specimen of each sex, collected July 11.

Habitat.—Popof Island, Alaska. *Type.* —Cat. no. 5253, U. S. National Museum.

This genus has not heretofore been recorded from this Continent. The present species would fall in the genus *Okenia* as defined by Becker (Berliner Ent. Zeitsch., 1894, p. 141), but as that name is preoccupied in the Mollusca, the species previously referred to it may be transferred to *Pogonota,* with which they agree except in a few trifling particulars.

Cordylura praeusta Loew.

Cordylura prausta Loew, Berliner Ent. Zeitsch., p. 96, 1864.

Berg Bay, Alaska: a single specimen, collected June 10. Originally described from Canada, and has been recorded from New Jersey. The U. S. National Museum possesses a specimen collected by Mrs. A. T. Slosson at Franconia, New Hampshire.

Cordylura vittipes Loew.

Cordylura vittipes Loew, Berliner Ent. Zeitsch., p. 272, 1872.

Metlakahtla, June 4; Berg Bay, June 10; Sitka, June 16; Yakutat, June 21; Popof Island, Alaska, July 8: Seven specimens. Originally described from Sitka.

Cordylura variabilis Loew.

Cordylura variabilis Loew, Zeitschrift Ges. Naturw., p. 326, 1876.

Metlakabtla, June 4; Berg Bay, June 10; Virgin Bay, June 20; Kukak Bay, July 4; Popof Island, Alaska, July 11: Seven specimens. Originally described from Massachusetts. Specimens are in the U. S. National Museum collection, ranging from New Hampshire to North Carolina, and westward to Texas and Colorado.

Orthochaeta pilosa (Zetterstedt).

Cordylura pilosa Zetterstedt, Insecta Lappon., p. 732, 1840.

Orthochcctapilosa Becker, Berliner Ent. Zeitsch., p. 101, 1894.

Metlakahtla, Alaska: A female specimen, collected June 4. This European species has not heretofore been reported from this country.

Hexamitocera cornuta (Walker).

Lissa cornuta Walker, List Dipt. Ins. Brit. Museum, iv, p. 1047, 1849.

Yakutat, Alaska: A male specimen, collected June 21. Originally described from the Albany River, British America.

Family Helomyzidje. Helomyza zetterstedtii Loew.

Helontyza zetterstedtii Loew, Zeitschrift Entom. Breslau, p. 37, 1859.

Yakutat, June 21; Popof Island, Alaska, July 8: Two specimens. This is a European species, first reported from this country about twenty-two years ago. Specimens are in the U. S. National Museum from the White Mountains, New Hampshire, and Ungava Bay, British America.

Leria leucostoma (Loew).

Blepharoptera leucostoma Loew, Berliner Ent. Zeitsch., p. 28, 1863.

Popof Island, July 10; Kadiak, July 20; Saldovia, Alaska, July 21: Three specimens. Originally described from Alaska. Specimens are in the U. S. National Museum from the White Mountains, New Hampshire.

Leria fraterna (Loew).

Scoliocentra fraUrna Loew, Berliner Ent. Zeitsch., p. 27, 1863.

Orca, Alaska: A single specimen, collected June 21. This species was also originally described from Alaska. It has been reported from Mt. Washington, New Hampshire, and the U. S. National Museum contains specimens from Ungava Bay, British America, and Laggan, British Columbia.

Family SCIOMYZID-ffi. Tetanocera plumosa Loew.

Tetanocera plumosa Loew, Entom. Zeitung Stettin, p. 201, 1847. Monographs Dipt. N. Am., 1, p. 121, 1862.

Virgin Bay, June 26; Kukak Bay, July 4; Popof Island, July 9 to 16; Kadiak, Alaska, July 20: Eleven specimens. Originally described from Alaska, and also recorded from Connecticut and New Jersey. Specimens in the U. S. National Museum indicate that this species occurs from Maine and Pennsylvania, westward to California and Alaska.

Neuroctena anilis (Fallen).

Dryomyza anilis Fallen, Diptera Sueciae, Sciomyzidae, p. 16, 1820.

Dryomyzapallida Day, Canadian Ent., p. 89, 1881.

Yakutat, June 21; Virgin Bay, June 26; Kukak Bay, July 4; Kadiak, Alaska, July 20: Six specimens. A European species, first reported from this country about thirty-eight years ago. It has been recorded from Connecticut and New Jersey. Specimens in the U. S. National Museum show that it ranges northward to New Hampshire, and also occurs in Washington.

(Edoparea glauca sp. nov.

Black, the halteres yellow; head bluish gray pruinose, the entire front brownish gray pruinose, only two vertical bristles (the anterior) present, ocellar and postocellar bristles present, two pairs of frontoorbitals; face in profile strongly concave, the clypeus unusually large and projecting the length of the third antennal joint beyond the anterior edge of the oral margin, cheeks posteriorly two-thirds as broad as the eye-height, third joint of antennae orbicular; body bluish gray pruinose, mesonotum largely brownish pruinose, five pairs of dorsocentral bristles, scutellum bearing three pairs of marginal bristles, pleura and legs destitute of bristles except at apices of tibiae; wings grayish hyaline, stigma and base of costal cell yellowish gray, apex of first vein opposite the hind crossvein; length 6 to 7 mm. Four males and three females.

Habitat.—Metlakahtla, June 4; Farragut Bay, Alaska, June 5. *Type.*—Cat. no. 5254, U. S. National Museum.

This genus was founded by Dr. Loew in the Zeitschrift fur Ento'mologie zu Breslau for 1859, page 10, and has for its type species the *Heteromyza buccata* of Fallen. Dr. Loew draws attention to the fact that in his original definition of the genus *Heteromyza,* Fallen stated that the vibrissae are present, but as a matter of fact, this is true of only one *(pculata)* of the two species which he places in it; *oculata* therefore must be considered the type species of the genus *Heteromyza.* About three years previous to the publication of Dr. Loew's article, Rondani had selected *buccata* as the type of a new genus, to which he applied the name *Heterostoma,* but upon discovering that this name had been previously used for another genus, he changed it the following year to *Heterocheila.* But this name was, in his opinion, too near to the previously employed generic term, *HeterocAeilus,* and, accordingly, eleven years later he again changed it to *Exocheila.* As the name proposed by Dr. Loew had been published about nine years previously, it will, of course, take precedence over the name bestowed by Rondani.

Sciomyza glabricula Fallen.

ScwmyzaglabriculaYKLixxi, DipteraSuecias, Sciomyz., p. 15,1820.—Schiner, Fauna Austriaca, Dipt., 11, p. 44, 1864.

Popof Island, Alaska: A single specimen, collected July 13. This is a European species, not heretofore reported from this Continent.

Family PSILHXE.

Psila levis Loew.

Psila levis Loew, Berliner Ent. Zeitsch., p. 40, 1869.

Sitka, June 16; Yakutat, June 21; Virgin Bay, June 26; Kukak Bay, Alaska, July 4: Seventeen specimens. Originally described from New Hampshire.

Family ORTALID.fi.

Melieria canus (Loew).

Ortalis canus Loew, Berliner Ent. Zeitsch., p. 374, 1858. *Ceroxys canus* Loew, Monographs Dipt. N. Am., i11, p. 128, 1873.

Fox Point, Alaska: A single specimen, collected "July 28. A European species, first reported from this country about twenty-seven years ago. It has been recorded from Alaska and Nebraska, and the U. S. National Museum contains specimens from Colorado.

Family TRYPETIDfi. Tephritis murina Doane.

Ttphritis murina Doane, Journal New York Ent. Soc., p. 189, 1899.

Popof Island, Alaska: Seven specimens, collected July 9 to 14. The type locality of this species is Washington.

Family LONCHfilDfi. Palloptera jucunda Loew.

Palloptera jucunda Loew, Berliner Ent. Zeitsch., p. 29, 1863.

Kukak Bay, July 4; Popof Island, Alaska, July 8 to 14: Eleven specimens. Originally described from Alaska. The U. S. National Museum contains specimens collected in Idaho and Colorado.

Lonchaea albitarsis Zetterstedt.

Lonchaa albitarsis Zetterstedt, Insecta Lappon., p. 754, 1840. Dipt. Scand., vi, p. 2351, 1847.

Sitka, Alaska: Two specimens, collected June 16. A European species not before reported from this Continent.

Lonchaea hyalinipennis Zetterstedt.

Lonchaa hyalinipennis Zetterstedt, Dipt. Scand., vi, p. 2350, 1847.

Yakutat, June 21; Virgin Bay, Alaska, June 26: Two specimens. This is also a European species, not before recorded from this Continent.

Lonchaea deutschi Zetterstedt.

Lonchaa deutschi Zetterstedt, Insecta Lappon., p. 753, 1840. Dipt. Scand,, vi, p. 2348, 1847.

Sitka, Alaska: Two specimens, collected June 16. This species falls into the same category as the two preceding.

Family SAPROMYZDXffi. Sapromyza brachysoma Coquillett.

Sapromyza brachysoma Coquillett, Canadian Entom., p. 278, 1898.

Muir Inlet, June 12; Sitka, Alaska, June 16: Twenty-seven specimens. Originally described from New Hampshire.

Sapromyza lupulina (Fabricius).

Musca lupulina Fabricius, Mantissa Insect., 11, p. 344, 1787. *Sapromyza lupulina* Becker, Berliner Ent. Zeitsch., p. 213, 1895.

Juneau, Alaska: Two specimens, collected July 25. A European species, first recorded as occurring in this country by Walker about fifty-one years ago. It been reported as occurring along the eastern part of this country from Nova Scotia to New Jersey. Specimens in the U. S. National Museum indicate that it ranges as far southward as North Carolina, and westward to Kansas and Colorado.

Lauxania cylindricornis (Fabricius).

Musca cylindricornis Fabricius, Entom. System., rv, p. 332, 1792. *Lauxania cylindricornis* Schiner, Fauna Austriaca, Dipt., 11, p. 95, 1864.

Lowe Inlet, British Columbia, June 3; Muir Inlet, June 11; Sitka, June 16; Kukak Bay, July 4; Popof Island, Alaska, July 10 and 11: Eight specimens. This is also a European species, first reported from this country by the same writer and at the same time as the preceding species. It has been recorded as occurring along the Atlantic seaboard from Nova Scotia to Georgia.

Family PHYCODROMID.

Ccelopa frigida (Fallen).

Copromyza frigida Fallen, Diptera Suecia?, Hydromyz., p. 6, 1820. *Calopa frigida* Zetterstedt, Dipt. Scand. , vi, p. 2472, 1847.

Kadiak, Alaska: A single specimen, collected July 20. A European species, reported as occurring in this country by Osten Sacken about twenty-two years ago. It has also been recorded from Bering Islands.

Ccelopa nitidula Zetterstedt.

Ccelopa nitidula Zetterstedt, Dipt. Scand., vi, p. 2473, 1847.

Kadiak, Alaska: A single specimen, collected July 20. This is also a European species recorded from this country with the preceding species.

Family SEPSIIXffi.

Sepsis referens Walker.

Sepsis referens Walker, List Dipt. Ins. Brit. Museum, iv, p. 999, 1849.

Lowe Inlet, British Columbia: A single specimen, collected June 3. Originally described from North America, without reference to any more definite locality.

Sepsis flavimana Meigen.

Sepsisflavimana Meigen, Syst. Besch. Eur. Zweif. Ins., v, p. 288, 1826.— Schiner, Fauna Austriaca, Dipt., 11, p. 180, 1864.

Saldovia, July 21; Juneau, Alaska, July 25: Two specimens. A European species, not heretofore reported from this Continent.

Family PIOPHIUD. Piophila casei (Linn6).

Musca casei Linne, Fauna Suecica, p. 1850, 1761. *Piophila casei* Schiner, Fauna Austriaca, Dipt., 11, p. 186, 1864.

Juneau, Alaska: Two specimens, collected July 25. A European species, first reported from this country by Dr. Loew about thirty-six years ago.

Prochyliza xanthostoma Walker.

Prochyliza xanthosioma Walker, List Dipt. Ins. Brit. Museum, iv, p. 1045, 1849.

Saldovia, Alaska: A single specimen, collected July 21. Originally described from Albany River, British America, and has been recorded from New Jersey and the District of Columbia. Specimens in the U. S. National Museum indicate that it ranges southward to Georgia, and westward to Texas and Kansas.

Family EPHYDRUXffi. Hydrellia scapularis Loew.

Hydrellia scapularis Loew, Monog. Dipt. N. Am., I, p. 153, 1862.

Lowe Inlet, British Columbia; Yakutat, June 21; Popof Island, Alaska, July 8 to 10: Six specimens. Originally described from the United States without any more definite locality being given. It has been recorded from New Jersey,

and specimens in the U. S. National Museum indicate that it ranges westward through Illinois to California.

Pelomyia occidentalis Williston.

Pelomyia occidentalis WILLISTON, N. Amer. Fauna, no. 7, p. 258, 1893.

Saldovia, Alaska: Five specimens, collected July 21. Originally described from Monterey, Calif.

Parydra paullula Loew.

Parydrapaullula Loew, Monog. Dipt. N. Am., I, p. 167, 1862.

Popof Island, Alaska: A single specimen, collected July 10. No locality was mentioned in the original description, but the type specimen was evidently collected in some part of the United States.

Scatella setosa sp. nov.

Black, the halteres yellow; head and body opaque, densely bluish gray pruinose, cheeks at narrowest part about one-sixth as wide as the eye-height, a stout bristle near junction of each with the occiput and two on each side of the face; mesonotum bearing three pairs of dorsocentral bristles, the anterior pair in front of the suture, no bristles nor hairs between the two rows of dorsocentrals behind the suture, in front of the suture with a strong pair of acrostichal bristles, and in front of these are three or four pairs of shorter bristles; scutellum bearing a short lateral and a very long subapical pair of bristles; wings grayish brown, marked with five rather small whitish spots, one in the submarginal cell above the hind crossvein, one near the base and another beyond middle of the first posterior cell, finally one on either side of the hind crossvein; length 2. 5 mm. A single specimen, collected July 21.

Habitat.—Saldovia, Alaska. *Type.*— Cat. no. 5255, U. S. National Museum.

Scatella stagnalis (Fallen).

Ephydra stagnate Fallen, Dipt. Suecia?, Hydromyzidae, p. 5, 1823. *Scatella stagnalis* Schiner, Fauna Austriaca, Dipt., 11, p. 266, 1864.

Yakutat, Alaska: A single specimen, collected June 21. A European species, reported as occurring in Greenland about fifty-five years ago. It has also been reported from New Jersey, and the

specimens in the U. S. National Museum indicate that it occurs as far southward as Georgia and westward to Arizona.

Family DROSOPHILIIXffl:. Scaptomyza flaveola (Meigen).

Drosophila flaveola Meigen, Sys. Besch. Eur. Zweif. Ins., vi, p. 66, 1830. —Schiner, Fauna Austriaca, Dipt., 11, p. 279, 1864.

Sitka, Alaska: A single specimen, collected June 16. This is a European species, first reported from this country by the.writer in 1895. It was recorded from the District of Columbia, and the National Museum also contains specimens from Connecticut and New Hampshire. The characters heretofore used for separating *Drosophila* from *Scaptomyza* have been rather vague and obscure, and in consequence the last-named genus has not been generally adopted. A recent study of this group has disclosed a well-marked difference in the disposition of the short, bristly hairs of the mesonotum; in *Scaptomyza* these hairs are sparse and are arranged in two or four nearly regular rows, while in *Drosophila* as restricted they are numerous and not arranged in two or four rows. This difference, taken in connection with the widely divergent habits of the larvae—leaf-miners in *Scaptomyza*, scavengers in *Drosophila*—will justify the separation of these two forms into two distinct genera.

Family OSCINU).

Oscinis carbonaria Loew.

Oscinis carbonaria Loew, Berliner Ent. Zeitsch., p. 42, 1869.

Metlakahtla, June 4; Popof Island, July 8 to 12; Juneau, Alaska, July 26: Seven specimens. Originally described from the District of Columbia, and has been reported to occur from New Jersey to Nebraska, and northward to Canada.

Chlorops sahlbergi Loew.

Cklorops sahlbergi Loew', Berliner Ent. Zeitsch., p. 51, 1863.

Muir Inlet, June 12; Virgin Bay, June 26; Saldovia, Alaska, July 21: Five specimens. Originally described from Alaska.

Chlorops producta Loew.

Chlorops producta Loew, Berliner Ent.

Zeitsch., p. 52, 1863.

Sitka, Alaska: A single specimen, collected June 16. The type specimen also came from Sitka.

Chlorops scabra Coquillett.

Chlorops scabra Coquillett, Journal New York Ent. Soc., p. 46, 1898.

Saldovia, Alaska: A single specimen, collected July 21. Originally described from Oswego, N. Y.

Family AGROMYZID.E. Rhicnoessa parvula Loew.

Rhicnoessa parvula Loew, Berliner Ent. Zeitsch., p. 45, 1869.

Kukak Bay, July 4; Saldovia, Alaska, July 21: Two specimens. Originally described from Rhode Island.

Agromyza neptis Loew.

Agromyza neptis Loew, Berliner Ent. Zeitsch., p. 50, 1869.

Juneau, Alaska: Two specimens, collected July 25. Originally described from the District of Columbia, and has been recorded as occurring from Massachusetts to Florida and Texas, and also from Porto Rico.

Agromyza lacteipennis Fallen.

Agromyza lacteipennis Fallen, Diptera Sueciae, Agromyzidae, p. 4, 1823.— Schiner, Fauna Austriaca, Dipt., 11, p. joo, 1864.

Saldovia, Alaska: A single specimen, collected July 21. A European species, not before reported from this Continent.

Phytomyza flavicornis Fallen.

Phytomyza flavicornis Fallen, Diptera Suecia;, Phytomyzidae, p. 4, 1823.— Schiner, Fauna Austriaca, Dipt., 11, p. 315, 1864.

Yakutat, Alaska: A single specimen, collected June 21. This is a European species, not before reported from this Continent. The U. S. National Museum contains specimens from Ohio and Illinois.

Phytomyza ilicicola Loew.

Phytomyza ilicicola Loew, Berliner Ent. Zeitsch., p. 290, 1872.

Phytomyza ilia's Loew, Berliner Ent. Zeitsch., p. 54, 1863. (Nec Curtis.)

Muir Inlet, June.12; Orca, Alaska, June 27: Two specimens. Originally described from the District of Columbia. The U. S. National Museum contains specimens from Massachusetts, California, and Oregon.

Napomyza lateralis (Fallen).

Phytomyza lateralis Fallen, Diptera Sueciae, Phytomyzidae, p. 3, 1823.— Schiner, Fauna Austriaca, Dipt., 11, p. 314, 1864.

Popof Island, Alaska: A single specimen, collected July 10. This is a European species, not before recorded from this Continent. The U. S. National Museum contains specimens collected in New Hampshire, Illinois, and Missouri.

Family BORBORILVE. Borborus annulus Walker.

Borborus annulus Walker, List Dipt. Ins. Brit. Museum, iv, p. 1129, 1849.

Popof Island, Alaska: A single specimen, collected July 10. Originally described from Nelson River and Albany River, British America.

Aptilotus politus (Williston).

Apterinapolitus Williston, North Amer. Fauna, no. 7, p. 259, 1893.

Farragut Bay, Alaska: Two specimens, collected June 5. The type locality of this species is the Panamint Mountains, California.

CPSIA information can be obtained at www.ICGtesting.com
Printed in the USA
BVOW06s0300040614

355172BV00028B/292/P